IDENTITY LOCKDOWN

Your Step-By-Step Guide to Identity Theft Protection

James R. LaPiedra, CFP®

ISBN: 978-1-4834-1627-4 (sc)
ISBN: 978-1-4834-1626-7 (e)

Library of Congress Control Number: 2014914216

Lulu Publishing Services rev. date: 6/23/2016

For our protectors, the heroic men and women who serve and sacrifice in order to keep evil and darkness from ever touching the goodness of our lives.

There are a thousand hacking at the branches of
evil to one who is striking at the root.
—Henry David Thoreau

Foreword

Many of you picking up this invaluable book will be unaware of the fact that identity theft has surpassed drug trafficking as the number one crime in the US. This is a sobering statistic—one that should put us on high alert.

The principal message of this important guide is, "Be vigilant and stay vigilant." And to do this, we need to educate ourselves.

Jim Lapiedra, an experienced ID theft investigator, information security professional, and financial advisor, has written a comprehensive and cogent guide to protect your personal identity—something he describes as a lifestyle choice.

The digital world we live in has unleashed significant new threats to personal security, including invasive voice and video surveillance, and the pernicious crime of identity theft. The individual has been left largely defenseless and vulnerable. This guide provides an organized and practical path to enhance your personal security. It steps you logically through what to do and how to do it.

Just look at the facts. Annual statistics show that identity theft, as the number one crime in America, causes $50 billion in losses to businesses and $5 billion in recovery costs to its victims.

It is most important to note that you can be attacked without your knowledge. And once you realize you have been attacked, you are likely to be engulfed in a quagmire of a criminal's making. The result is significant costs in time and money, not to mention the debilitating impact on your peace of mind and your reputation. The most upright of citizens have had their lives ruined by inheriting the criminal records of perpetrators of identity theft.

Get this guide, read it, and follow the author's practical steps for prevention. Key first on understanding how broadly thieves can mount their attacks. Then read the real-life stories that detail the attacks. The chapter on prevention talks specifically about how to organize your financial life and records, how to reduce your footprint, the importance of going paperless, and the risks presented by your computer. Oftentimes the solutions are as simple as employing strong passwords.

Next, the guide takes you through the important steps on how to self-detect and monitor all your financial accounts, the importance of your credit bureau reports, and how to read and correct them if they are inaccurate. Finally, if you find yourself a victim, the guide details each action you must take to recover and restore your identity.

I have read countless guides and other protection information on identity theft over recent years.

LaPiedra's book is far and away the most complete and authoritative on this critical security issue. I strongly recommend that you follow this intelligent and digestible guide. The information is organized to school, not to overwhelm— the latter being the trademark of many other books on this terrifying topic. If you follow LaPiedra's advice, it will help protect you and your assets, and provide significant peace of mind.

Ted Price
Former Director of Global Security, Lehman Brothers, Inc.
Former Deputy Director of Operations, CIA
April 2014

Preface

In the early months of 2012, my partners and I became aware that an increasing number of our financial clients were becoming victims of identity fraud. One of the many responsibilities of a financial advisor is to manage financial risk. This risk includes the tragic consequences of identity theft, which can ultimately lead to financial ruin.

Given my law enforcement and security management experience, I was compelled to find a solution to minimize my clients' risk and provide recourse if they were to fall victim. I quickly learned that many existing risk reduction and recovery services either were too limited in scope, were marketing programs disguised as security services, or were just complete "vaporware."

With nothing viable in existence, I realized that to provide clients with a comprehensive identity theft protection program of real value, I'd need to develop it myself.

I researched extensively, compiling a vast range of detailed information from the most credible resources available.

The result: *Identity Lockdown*, an in-depth guide to identity theft and fraud prevention, detection, and recovery. With best practices, case studies, step-by-step action plans, and countless resources, *Identity Lockdown* serves as an invaluable educational tool.

This rapidly growing epidemic has completely changed the scope of what's required in protecting ourselves. Gone are the days of relying solely on credit monitoring services. New vulnerabilities require individuals to be more proactive, vigilant, and self-reliant than ever before. Today's reality: *prepare* or *repair.* The choice is yours.

Writing this guide was not an isolated endeavor. I was fortunate enough to have the assistance of many people, to whom I'd like to offer my heartfelt gratitude:

My wife, Fran, for her love and unwavering support. My children: James, Alyse, Kristina, and Robert—*you* are my inspiration. I love you all so much.

Sabrina Cohen (www.word-ology.com), my outstanding editor and a true professional whose extraordinary creativity gave structure and life to my thoughts.

Hugh "Ted" Price, thanks for your meaningful guidance and valued support.

Robert S. Tucker, Esq., Chairman and CEO, T & M Protection Resources, for your valued advice and continuous support. Thank you, friend.

Contents

PART I: EDUCATION

PART II: ACTION

- Medical Identity Theft
- Phone Fraud
- Mail Fraud
- Passport Fraud

- The Fair Credit Reporting Act (FCRA)
- The Fair and Accurate Credit Transaction Act (FACTA)
- The Fair Debt Collection Practices Act (FDCPA)
- The Identity Theft and Assumption Deterrence Act
- Additional Federal Rights
- Additional State Rights

Introduction

Congratulations on taking the first step toward protecting your identity. Personal security is a dynamic process that only you can choose for yourself—but that doesn't mean you have to walk the road alone.

I've combined decades of law enforcement experience to produce this comprehensive, step-by-step identity lockdown guide. It delivers the education, awareness, tools, and techniques necessary to protect you and your loved ones from the ever-increasing risk of identity theft and fraud. Below is just some of what you'll learn in the pages that follow.

Here's what you'll learn:
- the different forms of identity theft
- the information criminals target
- how thieves steal your information and use it to commit fraud
- how to assess your current risk factors
- how to reduce your vulnerability
- how to proactively monitor for suspicious activity
- how to detect threats and breaches
- how to respond quickly to restore your identity
- about your consumer rights under federal law
- about the cases of real identity theft victims
- how you can access the latest information with our list of free resources

This guide will outline the many forms of identity theft and the serious consequences victims face. Some may be familiar, while others will likely surprise you. Reading this guide will broaden your awareness, arm you with protective measures, and teach you to be your own advocate in the war against identity theft.

Each section of this guide offers important information that deserves your attention. Approach it one chapter at a time so you can fully grasp and thoughtfully apply what you learn. Implementing these steps over time will help you put better habits into practice and develop an entirely new way of managing your personal security.

Identity theft protection is a lifestyle choice that demands ongoing vigilance. While no one can ever be entirely risk-free, implementing what you learn here will drastically improve your preparedness and reduce your vulnerability. My lockdown guide will help you take control and establish a solid foundation—one step at a time.

The Security Cycle

Prevention, detection, and **recovery** are the key components of your security. Every aspect of identity theft protection lies in that comprehensive formula. Knowing and utilizing these components will decrease your odds of becoming a victim and empower you to recover quickly if an incident occurs. The details of each will be highlighted in upcoming chapters.

Prevention

Prevention encompasses all the steps you can take to protect yourself from identity theft. I'll outline those steps in the coming chapters. What you need to know, first and foremost, is that preparation is by far your best weapon against the threat of fraud.

Detection

Detection is key in exercising damage control and preventing further harm if an incident of fraud occurs. The sooner a compromise is detected, the more quickly you can alert your respective accounts and the proper authorities—and the more power you have to take action.

Recovery

Recovery refers to the first and often crucial steps in assessing the details of a security compromise. It's the in-depth process of restoring your personal identity information as closely as possible to its original status.

The Top Three Risk Factors to Your Personal Security

There are three factors inherently threatening to any privacy protection program:

- **Apathy** is a lack of concern.
- **Ignorance** is a state of being unaware.
- **Inaction** is the refusal to act.

An apathetic attitude encourages the myth that the effort required to reduce your risk is too great, too complicated, or too time consuming.

In reality, the time, effort, and expense required to recover from identity fraud is far greater than that to prevent it.

When it comes to identity theft, ignorance does *not* equal bliss. What you don't know *can* cause you great harm. Unfortunately, many people simply don't take action even after they've been educated on the risks and consequences of identity theft. Perhaps they buy into the myth that it won't happen to them. The truth may be hard to face, but it's the truth nevertheless: When it comes to the threat of identity theft, it's not a question of *if*—it's a question of *when*. With the growing number of fraud schemes, advanced technology, dispersed global networks, overwhelmed law enforcement agencies, and limited proactive security measures, we can no longer deny our risk.

Now more than ever, we are our numbers. In today's digital world, much of our lives are reflected in terms of numeric identifiers. A thief with access to those identifiers can prove disastrous. Your protection requires awareness and vigilance.

This program breaks down all the necessary information and security measures into manageable steps. By following these steps over time, you'll weave them into your daily life and greatly reduce your risk of becoming a victim.

You can alleviate the threat of ignorance by getting educated about the dangers of identity theft. This guide can alleviate your sense of fear, helplessness, and being overwhelmed by empowering you with practical tools and techniques. However, no one can control your genuine concern or convince you to act. Only *you* can be responsible for your personal security. You've already taken the first step. Making the choice to commit—*right here and now*—is your next step. Let's get started!

CHAPTER 1

What Is Identity Theft, and How Big Is the Problem?

In this chapter, you'll get a general overview of identity theft—its definition, its prevalence, how your information can be used, and the potential consequences.

Identity theft is a federal crime that occurs when a criminal steals your personal information with the intent of using it to assume your identity, commit fraud, and/or access your benefits.

Identity Theft versus Fraud

In plain terms, **identity theft** is the act of illegally obtaining personal information. **Fraud** is the additional act or acts of *using* that information to commit crimes.

The Identity Theft and Assumption Deterrence Act of 1998 states that identity theft takes place when a person "knowingly transfers, possesses, or uses, without lawful authority, a means of identification of another person with the intent to commit, or to aid or abet, or in connection with, any unlawful activity that constitutes a violation of federal law, or that constitutes a felony under any applicable state or local law."

According to that definition, the **means of identification** can include your

- name, date of birth, Social Security number, driver's license number, official state- or government-issued identification number, alien registration number, passport number, employer identification number, or federal tax identification number;

- unique biometric data—fingerprint, voiceprint, retina or iris image—or other unique physical representation; or
- unique electronic identification number, address, or routing code; or telecommunication identifying information or **access device.** This includes any card, plate, code, account number, electronic serial number, mobile identification number, personal identification number, or other telecommunications service, equipment, or instrument identifier, or other means of account access that can be used to obtain money, goods, or services or to initiate a transfer of funds (other than a transfer originated solely by paper instrument).[1]

Your information can be used in many detrimental ways, such as the following:

- to obtain credit, merchandise, and services under your name;
- to obtain false credentials: immigration documents, passport or visa, driver's license, government-assistance ID, medical insurance ID, and/or restricted access ID; and
- to commit crimes using your name.

Prevalence

Identity theft is a very real, very serious problem in this country. Published reports estimate there were 13.1 million identity theft victims in 2013, resulting in over $50 billion in losses for businesses and around $5 billion in recovery costs for victims.

FACT	According to the US Department of Justice, identity theft has officially surpassed drug trafficking as the number-one crime in America.

---

[1] Identity Theft and Assumption Deterrence Act of 1998, Pub. L. No. 105-318, subsection (d) of section 1028 of title 18, United States Code, 112 Stat. 3007 (October 30, 1998), January 2013.

How Identity Theft Can Affect You

Identity theft abuses personal information in ways that have long-lasting consequences. Unfortunately, victims often suffer losses far beyond the monetary costs. Some victims' identities may never be fully restored, depending on the extent of the compromise.

Highlighted below are some of the greatest risk factors.

Loss of Time

While some victims resolve their problems quickly, others spend countless hours—anywhere from thirty to several hundred—repairing damage to their good names and credit records.

Loss of Money

On an individual level, identity theft can cost you anywhere from a few hundred to several thousand dollars, and that doesn't include the costs incurred as a result of time spent reconciling the incident.

Loss of Credit

You may be denied loans for education, housing, or cars because of negative information found on your credit report. Damaged credit can increase your insurance premium and even cause you to be denied insurance altogether.

Loss of Reputation

You may lose out on job opportunities and, in rare cases, even be arrested for crimes you didn't commit.

Loss of Personal Health Security

Your personal health and safety may be at risk if erroneous information winds up in your medical files as a result of identity theft.

Loss of Peace of Mind

Worst of all, most victims experience a great deal of stress and anxiety, and a sense of helplessness and vulnerability that often lingers long after they've resolved the logistical issues surrounding their cases. When a victim's most personal and private information is compromised, most are left feeling deeply violated.

Identity Theft Is a Global Problem

On September 29, 2001, the *Washington Post* published an article about a man being held in Great Britain under suspicion of training four of the terrorists who hijacked the airliners on September 11. He had been using the Social Security number of a New Jersey woman—who had died in 1991.

Law-enforcement investigations subsequently revealed that the attacks were funded in large part through fraudulently obtained credit cards. Investigations also found that nine of the terrorist hijackers entered the United States using false visas and stolen or fraudulent identities.

CHAPTER 2

How Thieves Get and Use Your Personal Information

In this chapter, you'll learn ways thieves obtain your personal information and how they use it to commit fraud.

Despite taking common precautions, you may be leaving yourself vulnerable in ways you don't even realize. Knowing how identity thieves operate is the first step in protecting yourself. Review the methods listed below and note where you can step up your awareness.

How Thieves Get Your Information

- Thieves **steal private information on the job** by hacking into records or by bribing or manipulating other employees with restricted access.

- Thieves **steal your mail**—bank and credit card statements, credit card offers, new checks, and tax information. Most mailboxes are full of valuable information.
- They **Dumpster dive,** rummaging through your home, business, or public garbage in search of documents with personal information to help them open credit accounts, take out loans, open utility or phone accounts, etc.
- They **shoulder surf,** peering over you in an attempt to retrieve your PIN as you make purchases or use the ATM. In some cases, hidden cameras and cell phones can also be used to capture this information.

- Thieves use **social engineering** to manipulate us into giving away personal information. They prey on our natural tendencies to trust and avoid confrontation, often pretending to be a legitimate source before tricking us into sharing valuable information.
- Thieves use **traditional methods** to steal your wallet or purse.
- Thieves **steal personal information directly from your home.** Unfortunately, in addition to traditional home invasions, thieves

can be friends, family members, contract laborers, cleaning-service employees, nannies, and other trusted people.

- Thieves **skim** to capture your debit or credit card numbers using a data-storage device. They may swipe your card for an actual purchase, attach the device to an ATM, or even install a hidden camera to capture your info.

*TIP Before inserting your card at an ATM or similar transaction device, determine whether the card reader is permanently affixed. Thieves attach skimmers over card reader openings to capture your bank information.

- Thieves obtain your information by **hacking** into your computer. Utilizing spyware, viruses, or hacking tools, thieves gain access to passwords, credit card numbers, bank accounts, and personal information.

- **Pharming** also utilizes hacking skills by secretly redirecting you to a thief's illegitimate Web site, where you're prompted to enter personal account usernames and passwords. These fake sites are often created to look like perfectly legitimate sites with company names, logos, and information.
- Similarly, **phishing** is when thieves send you e-mails appearing to be from a familiar source like your credit card company, bank, or brokerage firm. They often request that you "update" or "verify" personal information or fill out a form that includes passwords, usernames, account numbers, and security questions.

- **Social networking sites** allow identity thieves to befriend you, earn your trust, and get you to share private information. Some also monitor your activity to track when you'll be going away, so they can attempt to burglarize your home.
- **War driving** allows thieves to access your wireless Internet connection. You can take all the recommended precautions to secure your computer, but if you use an unsecure public network or don't protect your wireless network at home, all your precautionary efforts will be in vain. Thieves drive around neighborhoods using wireless network detection equipment to exploit unprotected networks.

How Thieves Use Your Information to Commit Fraud

Thieves can use your personal information in many ways.

- They may call your credit card company to change the billing address on your account. They can accrue charges on the account, sometimes to the maximum limit. Because your bills are being mailed to the new address, you may not know about the fraud until you're notified by a collection agency.
- They can open new credit card accounts in your name, run up the charges, and refuse to pay the bills, leaving you with delinquent accounts and the debt noted on your credit report.
- They can open phone, wireless service, and utility accounts in your name.
- They can open bank checking accounts and write bad checks in your name.
- They can reproduce checks or credit cards, or electronically transfer funds in your name, in effect draining your accounts.
- They can file bankruptcy under your name to avoid paying for outstanding loans, mortgages, and credit card debts.
- They can buy or lease cars or boats under your name.
- They can obtain a driver's license with the thief's picture under your name and official driver's license number.
- They can receive medical treatment under your name and policy number, resulting in outstanding debt and false information on your medical records.
- They can file a fraudulent tax return with your Social Security number, or claim benefits under your name.
- They can provide police your identifying information during an arrest and never appear in court, resulting in a warrant for your arrest.

---CHAPTER 3---

Forms of Identity Theft

This chapter illustrates the various types of identity theft. We'll highlight real examples of how thieves operate and the consequences victims face as a result.

Now that you have a better understanding of what identity theft is, how thieves get your personal information, and how they use it to commit fraud, let's examine the different types of identity theft and fraud. Some may be familiar, while others may surprise you.

A common misconception is that identity theft is mostly limited to financial accounts and credit card fraud. However, **non-financial identity theft** is increasing at an alarming rate.

Financial Identity Theft

Financial identity theft occurs when a thief unlawfully obtains a victim's unique, personally identifiable information—date of birth, Social Security or driver's license numbers, account number and PIN—and uses it to commit financially driven fraud. While the most commonly known form of identity theft, it only comprises approximately one-fourth to one-third of all cases. The driving force in a financial identity theft is money, whereas with **non-financial identity theft,** there are other motivating factors like disguising one's identity.

In cases of financial identity fraud, the thief uses the information to open new credit accounts, take out loans, gain access to existing bank and brokerage accounts, open checking accounts, and even take out mortgages—all in the victim's name. The thief may max out credit accounts and even deplete existing accounts.

Even if you're not held liable for the fraudulent activity, you're left with the daunting task of correcting the information and trying to reclaim your financial reputation.

A Connecticut man spent more than 2,000 hours reconciling the aftermath of a wild spending spree at the hands of a twenty-year-old criminal who stole his identity. The thief made purchases in excess of $265,000 over a span of four months, including items from Lowe's, Home Depot, Sears, and JCPenney. He also purchased two cars from Ford and both Harley and Kawasaki motorcycles. Even though the thief was apprehended, convicted, and sentenced to three years in prison, the victim was still responsible for dealing with creditors and debt collectors to clear his name and credit file after learning that he had been victimized.

TRUE STORY
From the creditors' perspective, you are
guilty until proven innocent.

You're required to prove that you are in fact a victim—not just a deadbeat. This particular task—known as **recovery**—is both time consuming and stressful for many identity theft victims.

In another case, a New Jersey man continued to be haunted by the fraudulent acts of an identity theft incident that occurred ten years prior. Despite ongoing efforts to resolve his case, creditors continued to notify the victim about unpaid accounts, loans, and medical bills. Each time he faced another fraudulent activity dispute, he felt distressed and helpless. In 2012, the victim received a notice from the IRS that it had already paid out his tax refund of $62,000 to someone else! Although the IRS acknowledged the error and promised payment of his refund in full, he's still waiting.

Criminal Identity Theft

Criminal identity theft occurs when a criminal misuses a victim's personal identification information during contact with law enforcement. This can have devastating consequences for the victim. Many have incorrect criminal records stored under their names in police databases. Some victims are even improperly detained or arrested. Others are fired or denied employment. This type of identity misuse is very difficult to resolve and most likely requires legal representation.

FACT | According to the US Federal Trade Commission, approximately 12 percent of identity theft victims must spend time correcting false criminal records.

A California woman—who was initially stopped for speeding—was subsequently arrested and jailed for three days because another woman fraudulently used her name. When the criminal was arrested for cocaine possession, she identified herself using the victim's name as her own. When she failed to appear back in court, the judge issued a warrant for her arrest. Once the police verified that the victim wasn't the criminal, they released her with the assurance that the warrant would be corrected. However, not only was the warrant not corrected, but the victim was arrested, jailed, or detained seven more times by five different police departments over the course of almost four years. One of those arrests unfortunately occurred in front of her children. The victim eventually sued the city of San Francisco before a judge finally vacated the warrant.

Unfortunately, these situations can sometimes have a negative domino effect.

> In another case, a man's stolen wallet—containing his driver's license, social security card, US Air Force ID card, and four dollars—wound up costing him much more.
>
> Seven months after the theft, the man was suddenly fired when his manager discovered that he'd been arrested for shoplifting. The issue? The man had never really been arrested. This was the first domino to fall.
>
> The man's manager abruptly entered the incorrect arrest information in an industry-shared database. This prevented the victim from obtaining a new job, earning income, and paying his bills. Eventually, he was forced to file bankruptcy—domino two. Soon after, the victim lost his apartment—domino three. He began living in his car, and eventually in the streets, until a Catholic priest graciously provided him with shelter and assistance. The victim was finally able to obtain employment at a local department store, but was sadly fired the first day, after a background check revealed an "undisclosed" criminal record—domino four.
>
> When the victim went to the local district attorney for assistance, he was shocked to learn that his arrest record included shoplifting, disturbing the peace, burglary, arson, and armed robbery—domino five. It eventually became clear that the identity thief used the victim's identification every time he was arrested. Adding insult to injury, the thief was never arrested and the victim was forced to legally change his name—the final domino.

Social Security Number Identity Theft and Misuse

As a key identifier, a Social Security number is significantly utilized in most identity theft cases. Your Social Security number is linked to credit cards, bank and brokerage accounts, government service programs, health insurance, and in some states, even your driver's license number. The fraudulent use of a victim's Social Security number can take the form of financial and non-financial identity theft.

The **financial** misuse of a victim's Social Security number to compromise bank and credit accounts, brokerage accounts, insurance policies, etc., constitutes financial fraud.

Non-financial misuse occurs when a thief applies for and receives Social Security, unemployment, Medicare, housing subsides, or other government benefits. The thief can also obtain employment and avoid paying taxes with a victim's Social Security number.

In December 2006, Immigration and Customs Enforcement (ICE) agents conducted federal raids at six Swift and Company meatpacking plants. They uncovered one of the largest cases of Social Security number misuse by illegal immigrants, arresting 1,200 Swift employees. ICE discovered the operations of several identity theft rings that had supplied fraudulent or stolen identities and the Social Security numbers of hundreds of US citizens.

True Story

A woman was taken aback after applying for a job at Target, only to learn that she was on record as having been previously employed there. While processing her Social Security number, the human resources staff uncovered records of employment at thirty-five different businesses throughout the country that had been falsified by an identity thief.

> In another case, a woman in Dublin, California, discovered that her Social Security number had not only been stolen, but had been used by 200 illegal aliens to gain employment. That left her with an astonishing tax liability of more than $1 million.

Tax return fraud is becoming one of the fastest-growing crimes involving Social Security number misuse. **Identity tax fraud** has resulted in more than $7 billion in fraudulent payments. In addition, the IRS estimates that over 940,000 false tax returns were filed in 2010.

The inspector general for the IRS identified one residence in Lansing, Michigan, as the source of an astonishing 2,137 fraudulent tax returns, estimated to be a total of $3.3 million in falsely granted funds. Further inquiries revealed that a single residential address in Chicago had filings of 765 tax returns, resulting in more than $900,000 in potentially fraudulent refunds. The US Attorney for the Southern District of Florida called tax fraud an "epidemic" and a "tsunami of fraud."[2]

The IRS reported that in 2012, it intercepted roughly 5 million falsified tax returns whose collective refund requests totaled $20 million. Given the ease of electronic filing—approximately 140 million returns are filed electronically each year—criminals can easily file fraudulent returns. With nothing more than a victim's Social Security number, date of birth, and wage/earnings amounts, a thief can receive thousands in refunds. Total costs are now in the billions. Some thieves bribe check-cashing businesses into cashing refund checks. Others have refunds downloaded to a debit card designed for people without bank accounts.

---

[2]   Alvarez, Lizette. "ID Thieves Loot Tax Checks, Filing Early and Often," *The New York Times,* (May 26, 2012), 27 May 2012.

In most cases, victims become aware after attempting to file their real returns electronically and receiving rejection notices instead. In these cases, the IRS recommends that you immediately file a paper return and a Form 14039 (Identity Theft Report). If the IRS determines you were a victim of fraud, you will be assigned an identity protection PIN. Although the IRS states that it is aggressively working to address this increasing threat and reduce the time it takes to resolve cases, it currently takes 180 days on average to resolve. You can reach the IRS identity theft phone line at 800-908-4490.

Driver's License and Identification Theft

After a Social Security number, the second most widely used identifier is a driver's license or identification card number. Years ago, the most common cases of misuse were by underage teenagers trying to purchase alcohol or get into bars and clubs. With the sophistication of today's technology, thieves can capitalize on system weaknesses to obtain these documents directly from the states' DMV offices, allowing them to make authentic-looking licenses and identification cards.

Armed with a driver's license bearing the victim's name and number, a thief can ruin the victim's driving record. The thief's driving offenses, suspended or revoked driving privileges, charges of DWI/DUI, and outstanding warrants are now all linked to the victim. The offenses linked to a victim's license can cause a routine traffic stop to result in an arrest, incarceration, and even jail time. Resolution isn't possible until his or her true identity can be verified, and most cases require the representation of an attorney—at the victim's expense.

In 2012, the Minnesota Department of Vehicle Services released information regarding the issuance of driver's licenses to individuals with false identification. Through initiating this project, it identified that upward of 23,705 licenses were most likely fraudulently obtained. As you can imagine, a lot of damage can be done when a thief gets hold of a legitimately issued state driver's license. Drivers around the country are discovering fraudulent activity when they renew their licenses through the mail and receive a card with someone else's picture on it.

Medical Identity Theft

Medical identity theft is a very serious and potentially dangerous form of identity fraud emerging at an alarming rate. In these cases, thieves utilize a victim's information to obtain medical treatment, prescription drugs, and even surgery. The costs can range from several hundred to more than a million dollars per incident. Beyond the financial repercussions are much more serious issues, such as the creation of erroneous medical files or the misinformation added to existing ones.

Inaccuracies in blood type, history of drug or alcohol abuse, test results, or diagnoses are now linked to the victim as a result of the thief's fraudulent behavior. These inaccuracies could lead to improper treatment, injury, illness, or even death. In addition, medical records are extremely difficult to correct. Unfortunately, the victims of medical identity theft are not extended the same rights and protections as victims of financial identity theft. Files are often shared with other entities—co-providers, insurance carriers, medical billing centers, hospitals, and pharmacies—making it almost impossible to correct the information existing on so many diverse networks.

A Utah mother of four was shocked to receive a call from child protective services stating that she was under investigation because her newborn baby had tested positive for methamphetamines—a truly disturbing call for any mother. Even more disturbing was the fact that the woman had never taken methamphetamines and hadn't given birth in years. Investigators questioned her employer and her family—including her small children. Investigators even threatened to declare her an unfit, drug-addicted mother and take away her children.

It was only when evidence revealed that an identity thief had used the woman's stolen driver's license to register at the hospital—where she gave birth to a drug-addicted baby—that investigators began to piece it all together. Unfortunately, that didn't stop the hospital from attempting to collect the $10,000 medical bill from the victim. Adding insult to injury, when the victim was later admitted to the hospital for a kidney infection, records reflected the blood type of the thief instead of her own.

The executive director of the <u>World Privacy Forum</u>, Pam Dixon, summarized these types of problems in her 2006 report: "Medical identity theft is deeply entrenched in the health care system. Identity theft may be done by criminals, doctors, nurses, hospital employees, and increasingly, by highly sophisticated crime rings. The report finds that medical identity theft victims need an expanded right to correct their medical files in order to recover from this crime and need more specialized consumer education that is focused on correcting the specific harms of medical identity theft."[3]

Identity Cloning

In this type of incident, the thief literally takes the victim's identity as his or her own, usually in an effort to conceal his/her own identity. All forms of identification are created using the victim's information. In essence, this creates a duplicate of the victim's identity. Aside from the task of correcting fraudulent activity, the victim is faced with duplicate files maintained by creditors and government agencies.

While investigating a license fraud issue, a Florida Highway Patrol trooper uncovered an identity fraud case that had been perpetrated for twenty-two years, resulting in an ongoing nightmare for the victim. The trooper's investigation revealed that the thief had assumed the identity of a Florida resident after stealing his wallet from his car in 1989. The thief obtained a passport, driver's license, birth certificate, Social Security card, and identification authorizing unescorted access to a port and military installation. During the years the thief was using the victim's identity, he was arrested for assault, had his driver's license suspended, incurred debts, and even had children—all in the victim's name. This resulted in the suspension of the victim's driver's license and required him to explain the thief's assault conviction when applying for a job as a corrections officer. As a result of the trooper's investigation, the thief was arrested and sentenced to ten years in prison, all the while insisting that the victim's identity was his. Since the thief assumed the victim's identity back in 1989 and has never revealed his real identity, it remains unknown. He's currently listed as John Doe in prison records.

---

[3]   Dixon, Pam. "Medical Identity Theft: The Information Crime That Can Kill You," World Privacy Forum Report (May 3, 2006), 28 May 2012.

In January 2013, an illegal immigrant finally pled guilty to charges that she had completely assumed the identity of a Texas schoolteacher—ending an ordeal that had lasted twelve years. The perpetrator used the teacher's identification not to only open bank and credit card accounts, but to assume her entire persona. The victim became aware of the fraud when she was turned down for a mortgage. The thief used the victim's ID to get a job, a driver's license, a mortgage, food stamps, and even medical care for the birth of two children.

In a strange twist, the thief actually claimed that the teacher was the one who had stolen *her* identity. The thief was so brazen that she countered the victim's claim of being an identity theft victim and sought a new Social Security number. Compounding her torment, the Social Security Administration turned down the victim's request and issued a new number to the perpetrator. This forced the victim to file her federal tax return using a special identification number reserved exclusively for illegal immigrants.

Child Identity Theft

Child identity theft occurs when thieves use a minor's Social Security number to perpetrate fraud. Most children receive their Social Security numbers at birth, so these numbers are particularly vulnerable. Most children *do not* and *will not* have credit histories until they're adults. A child's identity is a clean slate, and the probability of detecting fraud is low. Thieves can establish lines of credit, obtain driver's licenses, or even buy a house with the child's identity. This type of fraud often goes undetected for years, and by the time it's discovered, it may be too late for complete restoration of credit and character identities. The potential impact on a child's future is profound. It could negatively impact his or her chances of securing a student loan, a place to live, and even employment.

One afternoon, the mother of a twelve-year-old boy received a letter from the IRS confirming that her son's tax return had already been filed. This was odd, considering her son was a minor and she filed the boy's tax returns to report income from modeling jobs. After receiving the same letter the following year, she made an inquiry at her local IRS office, where she discovered that her son was the victim of identity theft. The boy's credit file included excessive inquiries, defaulted accounts, and addresses for residences at which he'd never lived. Unfortunately, this saga played out for years, resulting in hardships that plagued him through his teens and early twenties. He suffered greatly—threatened asset seizures, lawsuits, problems obtaining financial aid for college, collection notices, denials for credit, and actually having utilities cut off—as a result of his damaged credit file. Since the perpetrator was never caught, the odds are good that the victim will continue to experience credit difficulties.

In another case, it was revealed that a fourteen-year-old-boy from Kentucky had a credit history spanning ten years. The child's Social Security number was first used to commit fraud when he was only three years old. The suspect, who lived in California, financed a home for $605,000 and ran up thousands in credit card debt under the child's name. The perpetrator was never caught, and the child's parents were left with the enormous task of cleaning up the fraudulent activity from the child's credit file.

Synthetic Identity Theft

In this form of theft, identities are partially or completely fabricated. A thief may combine a real Social Security number with a name and date of birth completely unrelated, or he may use a fictitious Social Security number with the victim's real name and date of birth. This form of identity theft is rapidly growing and proving difficult to detect. A breach may not show up directly on the victim's credit report, instead appearing as an entirely new file or sub-file in the credit bureau. In these cases, the creditor becomes the victim. However, the losses incurred by creditors and businesses are eventually passed on to you—the consumer.

There are also inherent weaknesses in the credit review process that need to be addressed. Computer systems are designed to match a person's information using his or her name, Social Security number, address, and date of birth. In most cases, if the system's program doesn't get a match on several of these identifiers, it will reject the request. But in some cases, the program moves on and clears the request for credit under a new identity, and a new file is created. This allows thieves to establish credit for a person who doesn't even exist. The creditor suffers the direct hit, but that cost ultimately gets passed down to consumers.

Despite a fraud alert on his credit file, an Arizona man became the victim of synthetic identity theft. Using the stolen Social Security number along with a different address and date of birth, the thief was able to obtain credit. The victim eventually uncovered thirty cases of misuse involving his Social Security number.

Another crafty identity thief, with knowledge of the credit bureau processes, was able to use as many as 500 synthetic identities to acquire hundreds of credit cards. Before being arrested by the US Secret Service, the thief charged approximately $750,000 worth of goods and services over a two-year period.

Identity Theft of the Deceased

Even the deceased are not immune to the threat of identity theft. Someone with a criminal record, extensive debt, or the desire to make a new start can assume the identity of a deceased person and, in essence, walk away from his or her true identity. This is known as **ghosting.**

Thieves know that grieving families seldom notify creditors and financial institutions of a death in a timely fashion. This gives them time to clean out bank accounts, change beneficiaries on insurance and retirement accounts, and even establish new lines of credit.

Thieves also know that financial institutions and creditors receive notification of deaths through updates to the Social Security Administration's **Death Master File**. These notifications occur periodically—meaning a month or more could pass before the death appears on record. That gives thieves ample time to compromise a deceased person's identity.

The Death Master File is an online search application used to verify someone's death. It's a resource utilized by medical researchers, hospitals, investigators, pension funds, insurance companies, and federal, state, and local governments, as well as for individuals researching their family trees.

FACT	Nearly 2.5 million deceased identities are used each year to open credit card accounts, apply for loans, get cell phones, and execute a host of other financial transactions.

Because surviving family members are typically left to manage the estates of loved ones, they're also the ones left to resolve issues stemming from an identity fraud. A disturbing method is when the thief, utilizing pieces of the personal information of a deceased child, obtains a new Social Security number, driver's license, and other forms of identity in an attempt to assume the identity of the deceased child.

After suffering a heart attack, a Virginia Beach man was transported to Sentara Bayside Hospital, where he subsequently died. Several hours later, someone used the deceased man's credit card to purchase a laptop worth $1,800 at a local Best Buy store. Sadly, the perpetrator turned out to be a male nurse who attended to the victim in the emergency room. He was ultimately arrested and eventually pled guilty to credit card theft and credit fraud.

True Stories

A Georgia woman scanned the obituaries of eighty recently deceased persons, utilizing an Internet search company to obtain their Social Security and financial information. She then sold the information to people with bad credit for as much as $600 per name. It was later learned that the purchasers had listed the names of those deceased persons as cosigners on as many as one hundred auto loans at an Atlanta car dealership.

25

The true stories illustrated here are not meant to instill fear and worry. They are, however, real-life cautionary tales meant to make you fully aware of the seriousness of these threats and the potential extent of their consequences. I hope this new awareness drives home the importance of being your own advocate in protecting your greatest asset—your identity. I hope this new awareness motivates you to take action.

PART II

Action

Knowing is not enough; we must apply.
Willing is not enough; we must do.
—Johann Wolfgang von Goethe

Now that you've learned about the world of identity theft, it's time to turn education into action. Understanding how thieves operate allows you to think more critically about your own privacy. The most important element now is taking purposeful action to increase your chances of success.

Chapters 4–7 outline the steps you can take to reduce your risk. I've dedicated a whole chapter to each element of the personal security cycle— **prevention, detection,** and **recovery.** You'll also learn about your rights under federal law. Understanding these laws will empower you as a consumer and a citizen.

While this guide will provide you with specific steps, effective risk management requires you to take your privacy seriously. The only way to combat thieves is to stay one step ahead of them. The only way to stay ahead of them is to make privacy a habit as opposed to a one-time checklist.

Your risk management work will not end with the completion of this guide. From there, you'll be able to utilize the tools you've learned. Some will become second nature, while others may require time and effort to put into practice. The resulting framework will help you develop the most comprehensive risk reduction plan available.

The ultimate guardian of your identity is you. Monitoring certainly requires time and effort, but it requires *much less* time, effort, and stress than unraveling the chaos caused by identity fraud. And in today's world, it's no longer a choice—it's a necessity.

CHAPTER 4

Prevention

This chapter will show you how to measure and reduce your identity footprint, opt out of telemarketing and information-sharing lists, and take other proactive steps to protect yourself and your family from identity fraud.

Fear is for people who don't take action.

The fact is, no one can completely eliminate the risk of becoming an identity theft victim. Let's be honest—*that* fact can be a bit scary. The good news is that prevention is not about fear. Prevention is about taking control. The steps below will help you organize and inventory your information so you're as empowered and protected as possible. Our sample filing method will guide you through the process one step at a time.

Prepare

Like any good chef, prepping your ingredients before you cook makes for a successful meal.

Step 1: Purchase a Safe

A safe is a priceless investment—to protect not only against identity thieves, but also against fires, floods, and other unanticipated natural disasters.

- Choose a safe that accommodates hanging file folders, such as the Sentry Fire-Safe Security File Box or similar product. These locking, fire-rated safes are available for around $40 to $60.

- You can find fire-proof safes at major retailers like Home Depot, Lowe's, Sears, Walmart, and Costco. You can also purchase one online at Target, Best Buy, Amazon, or Overstock, or with specialty companies like <u>SentrySafe</u>.
- Visit <u>consumerreports.org</u> for an informative report on <u>choosing and using a home safe</u>.

Step 2: Purchase a Shredder

A shredder is vital to your protection.

- Purchase a quality cross-cut shredder for home use from an office supply store like Staples, Office Depot, or OfficeMax, or online at Amazon, Overstock, or Best Buy.
- Look for models that can cross-cut at least ten documents at a time, and shred CDs and credit cards.
- Although prices can vary depending on capacity and functions, a quality shredder for home use can be purchased for under $100.

*TIP	Keep your shredder close to where you normally open your mail. Get in the habit of shredding documents you don't need right away. **Remember**—trash is cash to thieves.

Step 3: Purchase Organizing Materials

I suggest purchasing the following items:

- multi-colored or multi-patterned subject folders
- hanging folders
- labels or a label-maker
- paper clips and/or small and medium-sized binder clips
- plastic protective sleeves for important documents

Itemize and Organize

Getting organized is not only smart—it's liberating. Taking stock of your information heightens awareness and empowers you to regulate its accessibility to predators.

The goal here is to make your information easy for *you* to access. In the process, we often discover we've been hanging onto things we simply don't need. Those things not only take up physical space in our homes, but take up space in our minds as well.

Step 1: Record and Reduce the Contents of Your Wallet

If your wallet is lost or stolen, this list will make the process of notifying your accounts, cancelling and reordering cards, and detecting fraudulent activity much more efficient—and much less stressful. What information would you *not* want thieves getting their hands on? Consider that thought every time you bring your wallet with you.

- Make a list of all credit cards, debit cards, store cards, and any other forms of identification.
- For even greater efficiency, record the contact number of each account so that you can easily contact them in the event your information is lost or stolen.
- Slim down your wallet. Carry *only* what you need for the day in your wallet or purse.
- *Don't* carry more than two credit cards.
- *Never* carry checks or your Social Security card.
- Photocopy all the items you normally carry in your wallet or purse.
- Store the list in your safe. Having an inventory will make it easier to cancel accounts or replace identification if this information is lost or stolen.

Fat wallet = **bad**　　　　Thin wallet = **good**

Step 2: Organize Your Paperwork

Clutter often creates chaos where there can be clarity. Remember—less is more.

- Gather your paperwork and personal information. Include all your important legal, medical, and financial documents:
  - driver's license
  - Social Security card
  - birth certificate
  - credit and debit cards
  - medical insurance cards and statements
  - passport
  - tax returns and records
  - wills and trusts
  - blank checks, canceled checks, and bank statements
  - insurance statements
  - brokerage account statements
  - utility bills
- Organize paperwork into piles by category or vendor.
- Label your color-coded folders accordingly.
- File each document into its corresponding folder—within each folder you may want to organize documents by date, starting with the most recent at the front.

- The originals of some important documents are best stored in a safe deposit box at your bank. We've noted those documents below. Make copies so you have the information on file at home.
- A safe deposit box is a worthy investment in securing your most vital documents. Granting access to your spouse (or one or two other highly trusted sources) makes these documents readily available in an emergency.
- Set aside any documents to be shredded or discarded.

Sample Filing Method

---

* The originals of all documents below labeled (*copy) should be kept in a safe deposit box.

Health (Red Folder)
These are the documents you may need in a medical emergency:
- prescription drug lists
- living will
- medical power of attorney
- health insurance
- emergency contacts

Banking and Investments (Green)
- savings accounts
- checking accounts
- taxable investment accounts
- tax-deferred investment accounts
- annuities
- safe deposit box information and key
- important contacts

Insurance (Blue)
- life insurance (*copy)
- additional policies (homeowner, auto)

Estate (Orange)
- durable power of attorney
- will (*copy)
- estate plan, trusts (*copy)

Important Documents (Purple)
- forms of identification
- marriage license (*copy)
- birth certificates (*copy)
- death certificates (*copy)
- adoption, divorce papers (*copy)
- inventory and photographs of household property
- deed to house (*copy)
- titles (*copy)
- mortgage documents (*copy)
- important Web sites/passwords
- credit cards
- Social Security cards
- tax returns and applicable documents for previous seven years[4]
- other important documents

---

[4] Consult your attorney or tax preparer regarding legal and tax documents—these have varying retention requirements.

Reduce Your Identity Footprint

We all have personal paperwork, account information both online and off, and important documents pertaining to our lives. Collectively, that information makes up our **identity footprint.**

Now that you've taken your identity inventory and sorted through your paperwork, it's time to lighten the load. Apply the steps below as you go through each category. Remember—the larger your identity footprint, the greater your risk.

Use the acronym **OPS** to help you remember each step. Where applicable, implement these three crucial steps to reduce your identity footprint.

1) **O**pt out
2) **P**refer paperless
3) **S**hred

Step 1: **O**pt Out

Opting out is an empowering proactive measure. It greatly reduces the number of times your information is shared, which in turn, greatly decreases your odds of becoming a victim. It can also alleviate the frustration of receiving unwanted solicitations.

Step 2: **P**refer Paperless

"Going green" is another proactive measure that can greatly reduce your risk. Since most accounts and financial records are accessible online, you can often eliminate hard copy delivery altogether. Check with each account company to see if they offer paperless statements—you'll be saving some trees *and* the hassle of managing more paperwork.

> ***Never*** handle personal or financial transactions using a public computer or while using your own computer at a Wi-Fi hotspot. Carefully review our section on the importance of protecting your computer.

Step 3: **S**hred Unnecessary Documents

Many documents we throw away are a treasure trove for identity thieves: account and policy numbers, medical plan information, balances, convenience checks, pre-approved credit offers, secondary addresses, memberships, etc. Protect yourself by shredding anything with personal identifiers and account information. Destroying all credit/debit cards, expired identification cards, and old statements you no longer need is essential to reducing your risk. When it comes to your mail, follow this rule of thumb: ***when in doubt, don't throw it out—shred instead!***

You're now ready to reduce your identity footprint. Each category below highlights the proactive measures you can take to offset the risk of fraud and theft.

Mailing Lists and Direct Marketing

The Direct Marketing Association (DMA) is a trade organization comprised of member companies that use direct mail, e-mail, and telephone marketing to solicit consumers.

Many major corporations mail pre-approved credit cards, loans, or lines of credit to consumers, hoping to attract new business. Most of these solicitations are sent via direct mail, where they can easily end up in the wrong hands. A thief with access can activate these offers and leave you liable for the cost until you prove that the activity is fraudulent.

> *Warning!* If an existing account is breached and the victim does not detect it for sixty days, the victim's liability is unlimited.

- Call 1-888-5OPTOUT (1-888-567-8688), or visit www. optoutprescreen.com to opt out of junk mailings, pre-approved credit programs, information sharing, and direct marketing campaigns. To **permanently** opt out of direct marketing campaigns, mail your request in writing to the company sending you marketing material.
- For all general direct marketing, **opt out** of mail, e-mail, and telephone solicitations by visiting the DMA (Direct Marketing Association) and requesting removal from marketing lists.

> **Note:** These opt-out services are only available to individuals, and not all businesses out there are members of the DMA. Check with each account for verification.

- Be sure to include your spouse and other household family members when opting out.
- **Prefer paperless:** If you'd like to remain on any lists, ask that they send you offers via e-mail as opposed to direct mail.

- **Shred** any offers you don't intend to utilize.

> **Important!**
> Sign all credit and debit cards.

Credit Cards

- Your signature is required by contract (read the fine print). Failing to sign your card could render you liable for any fraudulent charges.
- In addition to your signature, write "photo ID required" on the front and back of the card with indelible ink with a Sharpie permanent marker. Most cashiers won't even look at the card or signature, but a thief may not want to take the chance.
- Cancel any credit and financial accounts you don't use. This includes store cards (e.g., Macy's, The Home Depot).
- Ask for written or e-mail confirmation that the account has been closed.
- **Opt out:** For accounts you continue to use, request that your card issuer opt you out of all information sharing—including that with other businesses. They can, however, share information with their affiliates.
- **Prefer paperless:** Request that the issuer stop mailing convenience checks—which are very susceptible to theft. Ask to have statements e-mailed.
- Some issuers may require you to send your request by mail. Be sure to send it certified mail, return receipt requested. Save all copies of correspondence.

- **Shred:** Thoroughly shred any cards that are expired, cancelled, or no longer in use. Also shred convenience checks or pre-approved credit card offers.
- In addition, most credit card issuers have text alert services that can notify you via text message or e-mail when transactions, address change requests, or other activities occur. This proactive measure is a great way to monitor your accounts.

Financial Institutions

- **Opt out:** Request that all your financial institutions—banks, brokerage, insurance companies, and anywhere else you have an account—remove you from all information sharing.
- **Prefer paperless:** As with the credit card issuers, ask to have your statements sent electronically, thereby reducing the risk of mail theft.
- **Shred:** If you prefer hard copy statements, shred the prior month's copy when a new one arrives.
- Request a password on your account. Anyone making requests or inquiries on your account will be required to provide this password. This is a good way of layering your security. If the institution requires this request in writing, make sure to send it certified mail, return receipt requested. Keep copies of all correspondence.

See more about **strong passwords** under "Protecting Your Computer".

Telemarketing

No one likes the deluge of telemarketing calls that always seems to come when you're just about to sit down for dinner or relax on a Saturday morning. Opt out by placing your phone number on the **Do Not Call Registry.** It is maintained by the US Federal Trade Commission (FTC), and registration is free.

- Register by calling 888-382-1222 from the phone you want to register, or visit the Do Not Call Web site. To activate your online registration, you will need to provide an e-mail address so the FTC can send you a confirmation link.
- Once your number has been added, telemarketing companies have thirty-one days to comply. Although these companies are required by law to remove registered phone numbers, not all do. You may continue to receive some telemarketing calls, but that number will be greatly reduced.

Note: The National Do Not Call Registry does not prohibit calls from or on behalf of the following groups:
- charities
- political organizations
- legitimate telephone surveys
- companies with which you have an existing relationship
- companies to whom you have previously given written permission to call

---

- File telemarketing complaints online at the FTC complaint page or by calling 866-290-1222. Complaints or violations for individual states are generally processed by either your state's attorney general's office or the Consumer Protection Registries Division.
- Information regarding statewide do-not-call programs can be found on the Direct Marketing Association Web site.

- Due to the **Do Not Call Improvement Act of 2007,** your registration will never expire. <u>Learn more here.</u>

Data Aggregation Warehouses and People Search Sites

Data is big business. Companies specializing in data aggregation track, collect, file, and broker any personal information available to the public, essentially forming profiles on anyone. This <u>*New York Times* article</u> shares an inside look from a data broker's perspective.

Finding and regulating your information

- Perform a basic search of your name using Google and the sites listed below. You may be surprised at the amount of information accessible with a few clicks.
- Hundreds of sites exist. Removing all this information is virtually impossible, but opting out of as many lists as possible will reduce your identity footprint and limit the sharing capabilities of these sites.
- Many companies *only* allow opt-out features for victims of identity theft, persons who have been threatened and have filed protection orders with a court, political figures, and law enforcement personnel.
- Since each company has its own procedure, visit each site and review its privacy and opt-out policy. Companies make money on your information, so they make it difficult for you to remove your name. Given this fact, it's likely more prudent to follow the steps we've outlined in the Detection section: in particular, checking your annual LexisNexis report. LexisNexis is the largest data aggregation company. Here is a partial list of data brokers:
  - ➢ <u>www.beenverified.com</u>
  - ➢ <u>www.intelius.com</u>
  - ➢ <u>www.lexisnexis.com</u>
  - ➢ <u>www.mylife.com</u>
  - ➢ <u>www.peekyou.com</u>

> ➢ www.peoplefinder.com
> ➢ www.peoplelookup.com
> ➢ www.peoplesmart.com
> ➢ www.radaris.com
> ➢ www.zabasearch.com

Protecting Your Social Security Number and Card

Your Social Security number is your most significant identifier and should be used with an abundance of caution.

Who requires it, and why?

- Your employer and financial institutions may need it for wage and tax reporting purposes.
- Other businesses may need it to perform a credit check if you are applying for a loan, renting an apartment, or signing up for utilities. Sometimes, however, they simply want your Social Security number for general recordkeeping.
- Give your Social Security number only when absolutely necessary, and ask to use other types of identification.
- If your health insurer, school, or Department of Motor Vehicles uses your Social Security number, ask the issuer to substitute another number.

When someone asks for your Social Security number, ask the following questions:

- Why do you need my Social Security number?
- How will my Social Security number be used?
- How do you protect my Social Security number from being stolen?
- What will happen if I don't give you my Social Security number?

Answers to these questions will help you decide if you want to share your Social Security number with the business. If you don't provide your Social Security number, some businesses may refuse the service or benefit you want. The decision is yours.

> ***Do not*** carry your Social Security card unless you're required to use it that day. It's rare that you'd be asked to show your actual card.
>
> ***Beware of scammers.*** The Social Security Administration (SSA) will never contact you to verify your personal information for their records or continue your benefits.

Contact the <u>SSA online</u> or call 800-772-1213 to
* verify the accuracy of the earnings reported on your Social Security number;
* request a copy of your Social Security statement; or
* get a replacement Social Security card if yours is lost or stolen.

If you suspect Social Security number misuse, the buying or selling of Social Security cards, activity that may be related to terrorism, or attempts to obtain Social Security benefits, contact the <u>SSA Office of the Inspector General online</u> or by calling the **SSA Fraud Hotline** at 1-800-269-0271.

You can also access these SSA guides—<u>Identity Theft and Your Social Security Number</u> and <u>Your Social Security Number and Card</u>—or visit <u>this link</u> on the SSA Web site for more information.

Protecting Your Wallet and Purse

Many identity theft incidents occur using the information found right in a victim's wallet or purse—credit cards, checks, Social Security cards, and driver's licenses. Regardless of the amount of money in it, the loss or theft of a wallet or purse can cause much more than the inconvenience of replacing cards and documents. For a thief, the most valuable items *are* the cards and documents.

Despite that risk, we've all witnessed unattended wallets and purses on restaurant tables and bar stools, office desks, beach towels, and the dashboards of unlocked cars, as well as in shopping carts and gym locker rooms.

FACT | According to the 2010 Javelin Strategy and Research Report, "lost or stolen wallets, checkbooks, and credit cards account for nearly twice the amount of thefts as all online attack methods combined."

Protecting your wallet and purse can reduce your chances of being an identity theft victim by almost **30 percent**! Here's how:

- Minimize what you carry to only what you will need for that day.
- Limit your credit/debit cards to two.
- Don't carry your Social Security card.
- Only carry checks if you expect to use them for a purchase or payment that day.
- Bottom line—always be aware of your surroundings and make sure your wallet or purse is closed and concealed when not in use.

Carrying even one check is risky; a thief just needs your bank account and routing numbers to duplicate the check or access the account electronically.

Never enter your Social Security number, driver's license number, telephone number, or full account number on your checks. Businesses can verify your identification without those numbers written on the check itself. If they insist, consider what's more valuable to you—the item or your identity.

Protecting Your Mailbox

Identity thieves love mailboxes. They know the mail you receive contains enormous opportunities to commit fraud: pre-approved credit offers, convenience checks, account statements, annuity and insurance documents, and other forms of personal identity. This is why we strongly recommend receiving your correspondence via e-mail or online business sites. Discontinuing hard mail greatly reduces your risk.

These additional measures will help protect your mailbox:

- If you continue to receive sensitive items by mail, purchase a locking mailbox with limited space for mail deposit.
- Discontinue use of roadside mailboxes, if possible. Have a secured mailbox at your front door instead.
- Retrieve your mail as close to delivery as possible each day.
- Have personal checks delivered to your bank and pick them up there.
- Have sensitive documents sent via FedEx or UPS and requiring a signature.
- Mail sensitive documents at the post office during business hours. Do not use street mailboxes—not even the one in front of the

post office. These mailboxes have been and will continue to be looted by identity thieves.

- Consider opening a post office box to receive sensitive mailings.
- Monitor your mail. If expected statements and bills don't arrive, contact the sender to ascertain if fraud may be involved. If fraud is suspected, you will be able to take more timely remedial steps.
- If you suspect mail theft, report it immediately to the US Postal Inspection Service.

Protecting Your Computer

With the increasing popularity of the Internet, hackers are identifying and exploiting the weaknesses of various platforms. The following are best security practices that should be followed no matter what operating system you use.

- **Keep your firewall turned on.** A firewall is the first line of defense between your computer (and all the information stored on it), and the bad guys. Many operating systems have prepackaged firewalls. If not, review and purchase the firewall software best suited for your computer. ZoneAlarm, Norton, and McAfee are examples.
- **Install and update antivirus software.** Antivirus software is used to prevent, detect, and remove malware such as computer viruses, worms, adware, keyloggers, and Trojan horses. It's very important that you install an antivirus program on your computer and that you keep it current. Most programs update

automatically. If yours doesn't, monitor notifications and update regularly.

- **Install and update your antispyware.** Spyware is software that is surreptitiously installed on your computer to collect information about you without your knowledge. Keep your antispyware as current as possible.

- **Keep your operating system current.** Computer operating systems routinely update their technology and often include solutions to newly discovered security vulnerabilities. Updating to the latest version of your operating system is in your best interest.

- **Be aware of what you download.** Even the best antivirus protection software can be circumvented by malware embedded in e-mail attachments, pop-ups, and music or video links. Before opening this kind of content, make sure that it's coming from a trusted site. Never open e-mail attachments from someone you don't know.

- **Turn off your computer.** When not in use, turn off your computer to disconnect or prevent hackers from gaining access. Lock your computer screen when you step away—even for just a few minutes. As a backup, utilize the automatic screen-locking feature.

- **Engage your computer's GPS tracker (if applicable).** This new feature allows you to locate your computer in the event that it's lost or stolen. You may want to label portable devices "This computer has a GPS tracking device" to deter would-be thieves.

- **Back up your information.** Save the contents of your computer to an external hard drive. Backing up is essential for both maintaining your computer's contents and knowing what information may be in the wrong hands in the event your computer is lost, stolen, or hacked.

- **Use a secure browser.** When conducting online transactions or typing your private information, use encryption software. You can determine whether or not you're using a secure browser by looking for the small lock icon next to the URL or at the bottom of the webpage. Another way to determine if your communication is being securely transmitted is to check the URL scheme located in front of the web address—**https** is secure; http is not.

- **Encrypt financial and personal information.** Convenience factors like the amount of storage and ease of transport make computers, laptops, tablets, and Smartphones popular sources for your personal data storage, but it's for those same reasons that they're particularly vulnerable to theft. If you must store sensitive information on these devices, make sure you encrypt or password-protect your files. Invest in software that can encrypt your device's hard drive and wipe stored files remotely if your device is lost or stolen. Review comparisons of software products for your operating system.

- **Securely dispose of computers, printers, copiers, and fax machines.** Manually deleted information on your computer still exists on your hard drive. Many people are unaware that printers, copiers, and fax machines also record and store information that's been processed using those machines. To securely dispose of these devices, be sure to wipe their hard drives of all information. You can purchase software or bring the device to a professional to perform this service. If you're not planning to donate the device, remove the hard drive and destroy it with a hammer before disposing. Destroy CDs, disks, and flash drives before disposing as well.

  ➢ **Free hard drive eraser programs** can be found with a simple online search; however, many do not guarantee that all data will be removed, and most have limited (if any) customer support. Examples include Seagate DiscWizard Starter Edition, Darik's Boot and Nuke, Active@ Kill Disk, and BC Wipe. The following programs are available for purchase and download online for immediate use:

DataEraser, Drive Scrubber, Paragon Disk Wiper, Wipe Drive, CyberScrub Privacy Suite.

> **For computer recycling instructions**, contact your product's manufacturer or review the following: Environmental Protection Agency Computer Disposal Requirements, Earth 911: Computer Recycling and Reuse, E-cycling Resource Map.

- **Use strong passwords.** Here are some dos and don'ts regarding passwords:

  > **Don't** underestimate the power of your passwords. Since most thieves can easily access and authenticate the more traditional forms of identification—Social Security numbers, account numbers, dates of birth, addresses, and most commonly used security questions—a strong password really raises the bar of effort required on their part. I liken using weak passwords to using a knotted rope to secure the front door of your home—neither wise nor effective.

  > **Do** make passwords strong and unique for each account. They should be at least eight to ten characters long and contain multiple character types (lowercase, uppercase, numbers, and special characters).

  > **Don't** store your passwords on a list under your keyboard or blotter, inside your top desk drawer, or on a sticky note stuck to your monitor. I liken this to locking your door and then hiding your house keys somewhere on your front porch. Even though these actions are unoriginal and obviously not secure, people still do these things.

  > **Don't** create passwords using familiar or personal information like your date of birth, the last four digits of your Social Security number, nicknames, addresses, phone numbers, or the names of your children.

  > **Do** change your passwords every sixty to ninety days.

> ➢ **Don't** use the auto-memory features of a Web browser to remember your username and password.

Check your password strength at www.howsecureismypassword.net. For help generating creative passwords, visit www.safepasswd.com.

- **Secure your wireless network.** Prevent hackers from gaining access to your wireless network by enabling **Wi-Fi Protected Access 2 (WPA2)** instead of **Wired Encryption Privacy (WEP)**. WEP is more vulnerable against current technology. If you have an older wireless network device, upgrade or replace with software or hardware that supports WPA2.
- **Exercise caution when using wireless hotspots or kiosks.** If you need to access the Internet on the go, be aware that wireless hotspots and public kiosks often lack adequate security and are susceptible to adversarial activity. Use your cellular network, such as mobile Wi-Fi 3G or 4G services, or utilize a trusted tunnel to a VPN service provider. Limit your activity and never access services that require you to input usernames, passwords, or other personal information. Hotels, in particular, are becoming increasingly desirable targets for hackers. Their networks are notoriously unsecure, and in big cities, where lobbies are filled with high-level business executives engaging in sensitive transactions on their mobile devices, they can prove to be a haven for criminals. Always use a private VPN to ensure your protection.
- **Use security questions for additional access control.** Many Web sites require you to store answers to personal "security" questions. This is a good way of layering security, but, given the

amount of publicized personal information available via social networking sites, it's still possible for a thief to obtain the answers to these common questions. Providing fictitious answers can diminish your vulnerability. For example: When asked for your mother's maiden name, the street you grew up on, or the model of your first car, use false answers. Create a pseudo-identity just for this purpose so that the answers can't be traced using your real information. The key here is remembering your false answers!

- **Be alert for phishing and pharming scams.** Identity thieves use phishing and pharming to hack information. As defined earlier in chapter 3, **phishing** is an attempt to steal your personal information by tricking you into following e-mail links you believe to be trustworthy. Victims are led to a site that often looks identical to the ones they know and trust. Once on the fake site, however, they're directed to enter personal information, which is then captured by the thieves. **Pharming** is when a Web site's traffic is redirected to another site controlled by the hacker. As with phishing scams, once on the fake site, the victim is directed to enter valuable user credentials and personal information.

- For further information about securing your home computer and laptop, check out *Keeping Your Family Safe in a Highly Connected World* by Marie Baker and Jonathan Frederick. Parents should also check out this guide from the FBI: *A Parent's Guide to Internet Safety*.

Protecting What You Know: Social Engineering

Some thieves are bold enough to steal your information right out in the open, employing tactics like charm, impersonation, flattery, and intimidation to manipulate you into revealing information you'd normally keep under lock and key. The most common types of social engineering are in-person, phone, email, and Web site. Here are some precautions to note:

- Be suspicious of unsolicited phone calls, visits, or e-mail messages from individuals asking for or trying to verify your personal information. If an unknown individual claims to be from a legitimate organization—such as the IRS, the Social Security administration, or a company you do business with—try to verify his or her identity directly with the company.

- Don't enter information or use links embedded within an unsolicited e-mail. Be aware of whom you are communicating with, and always verify.

- Never be pressured into releasing your personal information.

- With companies you do business with, have the representative confirm information that only legitimate employees of that company would know, such as the date of your last purchase, the type of account you have, or when it was opened. You can even lie about certain activity such as purchase and payment activity and see if the unsolicited caller falls for it.

- In summary:
  - ➢ If you didn't initiate the call, get their information and call or e-mail back.
  - ➢ Stay in control of the phone call.
  - ➢ Know whom you're talking to and ask questions if you're unsure.
  - ➢ Don't be paranoid; be aware.

Example 1: You receive a call from someone claiming to be a representative of the Social Security Administration. The person informs you that the SSA suspects your Medicare number has been fraudulently used. In order to maintain continued benefits, you must confirm you're the authorized Medicare recipient by providing your Social Security number, date of birth, and your spouse's information. Fearful of jeopardizing your benefits, you cooperate. Playing on your fear of benefit loss and your cooperative nature, the thief employed minimal effort in obtaining your personal information.

True Stories

Example 2: Mrs. Smith, a seventy-two-year-old grandmother, regularly visits her senior friendship club at the local community center. One day, she meets Mary, a nice young lady taking a survey for a local children's charity familiar to Mrs. Smith. Mary reminds Mrs. Smith of her granddaughter. They talk for over an hour, exchanging stories about their lives. Sadly, Mary is an identity thief.

In their "friendly" conversation, Mrs. Smith reveals her date of birth; her address; her mother's maiden name; her husband's date of birth; all her children and grandchildren's names, schools, activities, and jobs; the name of her bank; even her medical issues and doctors—and Mary records every word on a small recorder in her shirt pocket. Mary even convinces Mrs. Smith to make a small donation to the children's charity. Mary claims to need her credit card or bank account number and the last four digits of her Social Security number "for security" reasons.

Think this could never happen to you? Consider how easy it is to let your guard down in social settings. Unfortunately, these scenarios and many like them play out every day in this country. The purpose of these stories is not to make you paranoid, but to make you more aware.

Protecting the Deceased

If you're a relative of a recently deceased person or the executor of an estate, the following steps will reduce the risk of your loved one's identity being used to commit fraud:

- Protect the death certificate as if it were a Social Security card.
- Request at least twelve original copies to show proof of death when closing down accounts.
- Request a credit report from each of the three credit reporting agencies. This will give you a list of accounts that may need to be closed.

- Request a flag to be placed on the deceased's file. It should read, "Deceased: do not issue credit."
- Indicate the person to be notified in the event someone attempts to open an account. This could be a surviving spouse, a family member, or the executor of the estate.
- Notify the following institutions:
  - Social Security Administration
  - insurance companies—auto, health, life, etc.
  - Veterans' Administration—if the person was a former member of the military
  - Immigration Services—if the deceased was not a US citizen
  - Department of Motor Vehicles—if the person had a driver's license or state ID card
    - Be sure to transfer any vehicle registration papers to the new owners.
  - professional licensing agencies—bar association, trade certifications, medical associations, union affiliations, etc.
  - membership programs—video rental, public library, fitness club, etc.

With a clearer understanding of the risks and consequences of identity fraud, you should now have a greater concern for the protection of your most valuable asset: **your identity.**

CHAPTER 5

Detection

In this chapter, we'll illustrate the importance of being your own identity theft watchdog. You'll learn how to monitor your credit, financial, medical, and social security statements, and the steps to begin taking if you suspect fraudulent activity.

Now that you've taken the steps we suggested in the previous chapter, it's time to discuss the next phase—detection. As with most things, being your own advocate is the most powerful form of protection. In their 2012 Identity Fraud Report, Javelin Strategy and Research—a leading independent research firm—identified proactive **self-detection** as the most effective method of detecting fraud; "It is in the consumers' interest to play an active role in managing their financial security and keeping a close watch on their financial activity."[5]

The Process of Self-Detection

Below you'll find information regarding various aspects of self-detection and the most effective ways to monitor and detect irregularities and fraudulent activity.

What is self-detection?

Self-detection is the process by which consumers actively monitor their own financial and personal accounts. Javelin's data showed that those who engaged in that process were able to detect fraud faster than any external source.

---

[5] Javelin Strategy & Research, "2012 Identity Fraud Report: Consumers Taking Control to Reduce Their Risk of Fraud," 17 (Feb. 2012), Dec. 2012.

Why is it necessary?

Early detection reduces the chance of further fraud and economic loss, in addition to the time and expense needed to recover. On average, it took twenty-four days to self-detect fraud, compared to fifty-eight days for external detection. Additionally, the average length of time the information was being misused was twenty-eight days when the fraud was self-detected, compared to sixty-five days when the fraud was detected by external sources.

That difference can have a significant impact on the amount of damage done to your identity and the chances of catching the culprit. Would you want your personal information in the wrong hands for even one day more than is necessary? Prevention techniques will greatly reduce the likelihood of having your identity stolen and fraudulently used, but no security measure is foolproof. The best security plans have layers. Self-detection is perhaps the most important layer in the mix.

Red Flags

The following "red flags" should prompt further investigation on your part.

- You don't receive expected bills or other mail.
- You see withdrawals from your bank account that you can't explain.
- Merchants refuse your checks.
- Debt collectors call you about debts that aren't yours.
- You find unfamiliar accounts or charges on your credit report.
- Medical providers bill you for services you didn't utilize.
- Your health plan rejects your legitimate medical claim because the records show you've reached your benefit limit.
- A health plan won't cover you because your medical records show a condition you don't have.
- The IRS notifies you that more than one tax return has been filed in your name, or that your file shows income from an employer you don't work for.

- You get a notice that your information was compromised by a data breach at a company where you do business or have an account.

Credit Bureaus, Credit Reports, and Credit Scores

Credit bureaus are companies that collect and compile detailed financial activities, credit ratings, and credit-related payment histories for every consumer in the country.

There are three main credit bureaus in the United States:
- Experian
- Equifax
- TransUnion

Innovis is a fourth credit bureau that functions as more of a data broker, but due to the amount of data they collect, any requests made to the three main credit bureaus should be made to them as well.

Your **credit report** is a profile detailing your extensive financial history and your activity with banks, lenders, and credit companies. The information contained in your report is extremely important. Credit bureaus use it to determine your **credit score**—a numerical rating reflecting your overall creditworthiness. Thousands of factors combine to determine your credit score, and each of the credit bureaus has its own calculation method. Therefore, your credit score may vary from one bureau to the next. Some major credit lenders have also developed their own scoring systems. The FICO score is the most widely known and used calculation model.

How is this information used, and why is it so important?

Your credit report and score determine your approval, interest rate, and credit limit for loans, credit cards, and insurance premiums. Companies use your credit score to evaluate their potential risk in lending you money.

They also use credit scores to determine which customers are likely to bring in the most revenue. Some companies will purchase reports from the credit bureaus to target customers they find to be desirable.

Typically, a desirable candidate is one whose track record shows that he or she is likely to pay bills in a timely fashion. The factors most commonly known to negatively impact your credit score are bankruptcy, late payments, unpaid debt, and access to too much credit.

Your credit report and score can determine whether or not you get approved for a mortgage, a car, and even a job. Prospective employers, landlords, and even your mobile phone company may utilize your credit report to determine your eligibility as an employee, tenant, or worthy customer. In their eyes, previous debts may mean you're an unreliable candidate. For employers, it may even mean you're more likely to resort to theft.

FACT	<u>A Federal Trade Commission study</u> revealed that one in five credit reports contain errors, and that 5.2 percent of those errors are so inaccurate that adverse decisions could be made as a result.

Why do I need to monitor my credit report?

Routinely monitoring your credit report greatly enhances your odds of early fraud detection. It also allows you to catch and correct inaccurate information that could negatively affect your credit rating.

How can I access and monitor my credit report?

- You are entitled to one **free** credit report every twelve months (not every calendar year) from each of the credit reporting agencies.
- We recommend staggering your free report requests—one every four months—from each of the credit bureaus over the course of a year (e.g., Experian in January, Equifax in May, and TransUnion

in September). You should also order from Innovis at some point during the year. Staggering allows you to monitor your files consistently and frequently over time.

Ordering your Free Credit Report

- Order **online** at www.annualcreditreport.com. There are many imposter sites used to commit fraud, as well as marketers trying to sell services you don't need. Do not use any other Web sites for this purpose. Innovis does not accept online requests.
- Order **by phone** from Experian, Equifax, and TransUnion, call 1-877-322-8228. For Innovis, call 1-800-540-2505.
- Order **by mail.** Carefully follow each site's instructions for documents to include.

Experian, Equifax, and TransUnion:	Innovis:
Download the annual credit report request form. Print, complete, and mail to this address:	Download the request form. Print, complete, and mail to this address:
Annual Credit Report Request Service PO Box 105281 Atlanta, GA 30348-5281	Innovis Attention: Consumer Assistance PO Box 1358 Columbus, OH 43216-1358

Reading Your Credit Report

Become familiar with each credit bureau's report format. Instructions on reviewing the information will be provided, but listed below is the general information you'll find on your reports. This type of information is reported for seven years. Bankruptcies, however, are reported for ten years.

Personal Information
- your name/variations used
- current and former addresses
- current and former employers

Account History
- creditors and account numbers
- types of accounts and terms
- dates opened
- highest credit, credit limits, or loan amounts
- balances, past due amounts, and account statuses
- payment histories
- dates reported

Public Records
- bankruptcies
- judgments
- tax liens
- state and county records
- foreclosures

> It's common for a credit account or loan to be carried under a different division or an affiliated company whose name you may not recognize. Verify the account and creditor before taking action consistent with fraud.
>
> If you do suspect fraud, immediately notify all three credit bureaus of any discrepancies or red flags, starting with the one that provided the report. We'll highlight further information regarding disputing and correcting credit file information in the upcoming chapter, Recovery.

Credit Inquiries, Fraud Alerts, and Credit Freezes

Credit inquiries list all parties who have accessed your credit report within the past two years. There are two types of inquiries: **hard inquiries** and **soft inquiries.** Hard inquiries are those made by lenders who evaluate your information when you apply for credit. Soft inquiries are those made by lenders for promotional purposes. There are two types of **fraud alerts:** an **initial alert** and an **extended alert.**

Initial Fraud Alerts

- An initial fraud alert can be placed on your credit report if you're a victim of identity theft, or if you suspect you may become one (e.g., you've received collection notices for accounts you didn't open, or you've provided your Social Security number or other personal information to someone you now believe to be fraudulent).
- When an initial fraud alert is placed on your credit file, you're automatically "opted out" of pre-approved credit and insurance offers for a period of two years.
- You're also entitled to one free credit report from each of the three major bureaus in addition to the standard one available every twelve months.
- An initial fraud alert remains on your credit report for ninety days unless you request to remove it before that period.
- Once the initial fraud alert is in place, creditors must use "reasonable policies and procedures" to verify your identity before issuing credit in your name, though these vary from creditor to creditor.

Extended fraud alerts

- An extended fraud alert remains on your credit report for seven years unless you request removal during that period.
- You're allowed to place an extended fraud alert on your credit report if you are a victim of identity theft and can provide an

Identity Theft Report—the <u>Identity Theft Complaint Report</u> filed with the Federal Trade Commission, along with a police report.

- Creditors are required to contact you when you have an extended fraud alert. Be sure to include your cell number in your contact information.
- With an extended fraud alert, you're entitled to two additional free credit reports within twelve months from all three major credit bureaus.
- The credit reporting agencies will remove your name from prescreened credit offers for five years unless you request to remain on their marketing lists.

> There is no law requiring creditors to perform a check with credit reporting agencies before issuing credit.

What Are the Limitations of Fraud Alerts?

Initial and extended fraud alerts are valuable measures of protection, but they do have limitations:

- Fraud alerts can help keep an identity thief from opening new accounts in your name, but they won't stop a thief opening new accounts that don't require a credit check—a telephone, wireless, or bank account.
- Fraud alerts will not protect you against nonfinancial fraud—driver's license, criminal, and medical identity fraud.
- Fraud alerts will not protect you from someone compromising an existing account.

What Is a Credit Freeze?

Most states have laws allowing you to restrict access to your credit report, also known as a **credit freeze.** This measure greatly reduces the chances of a thief opening a new account in your name.

- A security freeze is something you can do *before* an identity thief strikes.

- When you freeze your credit reports, you are telling the three major consumer reporting companies to block access to your credit report and credit score.

- A freeze works because most businesses won't open new credit accounts without first checking the consumer's credit history. So, once you place a freeze on your credit, *new* creditors will not be allowed access to your credit report. If your credit files are frozen, even someone who has stolen your Social Security number or other personal identifying information will have a hard time getting credit in your name.

- Companies you already do business with, and the collection agencies working with them, are still allowed access to your credit report so they can check your credit until your loan or business with them is resolved. Non-lenders like potential employers, insurance carriers, and landlords are also allowed access to your credit report in some states.

- Placing a freeze on your credit report does not prevent you from getting your free annual report or obtaining your credit score.

- Most states allow identity theft victims to place credit freezes on their credit reports for free, and only charge a fee for unfreezing the report.

- Most states require a filing fee for non-victims to freeze and unfreeze their credit reports.

- You are allowed to temporarily or permanently unfreeze your credit report at any time. For example: Before applying for a credit card or a loan, unfreeze your credit report by providing each credit bureau with the PIN given to you at the time of the initial freeze. A fee is normally required for each agency to lift the credit freeze. There's also a fee to reactivate the freeze once you've completed the credit application process.

For further information, review these <u>credit freeze articles on the Consumers Union Web site</u>.

For links to individual state laws and requirements, visit the <u>World Privacy Forum Web site</u>.

What Are the Limitations of Credit Freezes?

- Like fraud alerts, credit freezes are effective at preventing thieves from opening new accounts in your name, but not against other types of financial and nonfinancial identity fraud.
- They won't prevent thieves from committing fraud with an existing account or from opening new accounts with creditors who don't check the credit bureaus. With the latter, even if you're absolved of any liability, you're still left with the time and expense of resolving the fraud.

Credit Reports and Minor Children

Children are becoming targets of identity theft at an alarming rate. In 2011, the first ever large-scale child ID theft report revealed that 10.2 percent of children had someone else using their Social Security numbers and a 51 percent higher attack rate than adults. Parents and guardians need to be more vigilant in protecting children's identities.

"Child IDs were used to purchase homes and automobiles, open credit card accounts, secure employment, and obtain driver's licenses. The largest fraud—$725,000—was committed against a sixteen-year-old girl. The youngest victim was five months old."[6]

---

[6]   Power, Richard. "<u>Child Identity Theft</u>," Carnegie Mellon CyLab, (n.d.), Dec. 2012.

What should you do if you suspect fraud of a minor child?

- Minor children shouldn't have credit histories. However, if you suspect they may be victims of fraud, you should request their credit histories. If one exists, request the child's free copy of the credit report. You can also request a fraud alert or security freeze be placed on the file.

- Continue to monitor for suspicious activity involving your children, such as pre-proved credit offers, debt collection notices, or statements from creditors. Many parents mistakenly believe these items are just errors and discard them. These "red flags" require further inquiry to determine if any fraudulent activity has occurred using the child's information.

- Frequent inquiries on a child's credit record could cause a report to be unnecessarily created, thereby making it easier for a thief to obtain credit under the child's record.

- Make inquiries only when you suspect suspicious activity, or about a year or two before the child begins applying for his or her own credit. This will allow time to address any issues that might exist.

For further guidance in monitoring your child's credit, review the Federal Trade Commission's guide *Safeguarding Your Child's Future* and the Identity Theft Resource Center's <u>Identity Theft and Children Fact Sheet</u>.

Monitor Your Monthly Account Statements

- At least once per month, review your bank, credit card, utility, brokerage, and annuity statements. As we've mentioned, electronic statements are the safest, most effective, and most efficient way to view activity and detect fraud. They also eliminate the threat of mail theft.

- Review each transaction and verify the legitimacy of all recoded activity. If you're receiving hard copies in the mail, consider scanning paper statements, storing them in encrypted files on your computer, and then shredding the paper statement.

- **Account alerts** have proven to be very effective in detecting fraudulent activity in real time. Most credit card companies provide alert services—via phone, e-mail, text, or all three—to notify you when certain predetermined conditions are met. Alert conditions may include purchases above a certain amount, change requests, activity within certain time periods, or even general transactions. Utilize this feature on credit cards, checking accounts, and debit accounts. Some even offer the service for free—a sensible alternative to paying for credit monitoring on just one card.

Monitor Your Social Security Statements

- You should review your Social Security account statement every year. It provides your record of yearly earnings and your expected retirement and disability benefits. The Social Security Administration no longer mails these statements to you.
- You should open an account with the Social Security Administration online (800-772-1213) and access your information anytime.
- Verify the accuracy of your record. If your Social Security number has been stolen, someone could be receiving benefits from your account.
- Identity theft using Social Security numbers to electronically file false tax returns is becoming increasingly common. Social Security number misuse should be reported to the Social Security Administration Office of the Inspector General.
- Visit the IRS Web site and type in "identity theft" for the latest information.

Monitor Your Medical Reports

- For early detection of fraud, actively monitor your medical, insurance, and financial records. Unlike credit information that has a central repository with the credit bureaus, medical information is dispersed and maintained within many file systems and stored on numerous computers. This makes it extremely difficult, if not impossible, to locate and correct any errors or fraudulent entries.
- According to the FTC, these may be **warning signs of medical identity theft:**
    - ➤ You are contacted or receive bills for medical services you never got.
    - ➤ You see medical collection notices you don't recognize on your credit report.
    - ➤ You find unexplained office visits and treatments on the explanation of benefits statement from your health insurance company.
    - ➤ You try to make a legitimate insurance claim and your health plan says you've reached your benefit limit.
    - ➤ You're denied insurance because your medical records show a condition you don't have.[7]

Monitor Your Explanation of Benefits (EOB) Statement

- Carefully read the explanation of benefits (EOB) statement sent by your health insurance company after treatment.
- Verify that the claims paid, names of providers, dates of service, and itemized list of treatments match what you or your family members received.

---

[7] Bureau of Consumer Protection Business Center, <u>Medical Identity Theft: FAQs for Health Care Providers and Health Plans</u>, (Jan. 2011), Jan. 2013.

- Contact your health insurance company if you detect any discrepancies. If you suspect fraud, follow the instructions detailed in the upcoming Recovery section of this guide.

Monitor Your Medical Records

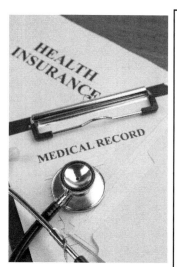

The Health Insurance Portability and Accountability Act's (HIPAA) Privacy, Security, and Breach Notification Rules help protect the privacy of your health information held by doctors, nurses, pharmacies, hospitals, clinics, nursing homes, health insurance companies, health maintenance organizations (HMOs), employer group health plans, and certain government programs that pay for health care, including Medicare and Medicaid.

- The provisions in the act give you the right to obtain copies of your medical records maintained by health insurance companies and medical providers. Generally, once you submit your request, these providers are required to comply within thirty days.
- Each health insurance provider requires a request form and fee for processing. Again, since there is no central repository for medical records, you will have to file requests with each plan and medical provider you use. This includes health insurance companies, doctors, dentists, clinics, hospitals, labs, and pharmacies.
- For further information on obtaining, protecting, and correcting your medical records, contact the World Privacy Forum—a nonprofit, non-partisan public interest research group. As the

only one of its kind conducting independent and original work, the organization focuses on in-depth research, analysis, and consumer education around the issue of privacy. The <u>Center on Medical Rights and Privacy Health Policy Institute</u> is also a valuable source of information on consumers' rights to their own medical records and privacy protections.

- If you believe your rights under HIPAA have been violated, <u>file a complaint with the US Department of Health and Human Services</u>.

Monitor Your Driver's License Record

- Although advanced security measures are taken to detect fraudulent driver's license applications, identity thieves are still able to obtain them with stolen identities.
- Becoming a victim could result in mounting tickets and even outstanding arrest warrants in your name.
- Monitor your driving record with your state's DMV. Most requests can be made on your state's official Web site. Links to each state's DMV can be found <u>here</u>. Be aware that states do charge a minimal fee for this request.
- If your state uses your Social Security number as your driver's license number, ask to substitute another identifier. If you suspect that someone has obtained a driver's license utilizing your personal information, contact your local DMV immediately.

Monitor Your Investment Account Statements

- In addition to password protecting your investment accounts, closely monitor your brokerage and annuity statements for fraudulent activity.
- Immediately contact your account manager for an explanation of questionable activity.

- Visit the Securities and Exchange Commission (SEC) Web site for <u>detailed information on investor fraud</u>. If you suspect fraud, file an <u>investor complaint</u> or visit the <u>Office of Investors Education and Assistance</u>. They provide assistance to investors wanting to report possible investment fraud or the mishandling of their investments by securities professionals.

Monitor Your Phone Bills

- Carefully review the monthly activity reported on your home and cell phone bills. If you suspect fraudulent activity, contact your provider for an explanation of the suspected activity.
- Be aware that just because the provider corrects the billing information, it doesn't mean your problem has been resolved. This activity should be considered a red flag warranting further review of your credit reports and personal records, as detailed in this section.

Monitor Specialty Consumer Reports

- A specialty consumer report is a non-credit report available to anyone inquiring about a consumer's background for decision-making purposes.
- These reports are compiled from thousands of public record databases across the country. These databases apply advanced algorithms to observe, record, and make inferences about your behavior. They contain the detailed personal information you've essentially generated since birth—insurance claims, residential and tenant history, criminal background, employment history, checking account history, e-mail accounts, online purchases, credit applications, and employment and education history.
- Companies like Google and Facebook use these new technologies to make business decisions and possibly predict how you, the user of their software, will respond to certain situations. These "big

data" sources have raised some privacy concerns. Remember—you are not the customer of these social networking sites; *the advertisers are the customers,* and your information and online behavior are what they want.

- Reviewing these reports annually is critical given all that they cover. You're entitled to one free copy every twelve months, just like your credit report. You also have the right to dispute inaccurate information.

- With hundreds of companies compiling data, it's virtually impossible to redact your identity from them all. Be wary of any services claiming otherwise, and focus instead on reviewing the following records thoroughly to improve your odds of protection. Each is available to you for free.

Background Check Reports

LexisNexis is the largest private sector data warehouse in the United States, maintaining approximately 37 billion public and proprietary records. These records are compiled into specialty reports and sold to businesses making decisions relative to background screening, employment and tenant history, and insurance underwriting. FACTA allows you one free copy of each report every twelve months. LexisNexis provides two specific reports containing personal information gathered from many different sources:

The first is the **LexisNexis Accurint Person Report.**
- It provides both public and non-public information—real estate title records, liens, death records, and motor vehicle registrations.
- Publicly available information is gathered from general public and non-government sources, such as newspapers, magazine articles, and telephone directories.
- Non-public information includes current and former addresses, Social Security numbers, previous names used—aliases, maiden

names, and previous married names—as well as dates of birth and telephone numbers.

- Order your <u>LexisNexis Accurint Persons Report online</u> or print and mail the completed form to this address:

    LexisNexis Risk Solutions FL, Inc.
    Accurint Consumer Inquiry Department
    PO Box 105610
    Atlanta, GA 30348-105610

- Include a copy (never send originals) of one of the following documents:
    - ➢ driver's license (non-expired)
    - ➢ state-issued ID card (non-expired)
    - ➢ Social Security card
- You must also include one of the following documents as proof of name and mailing address:
    - major bank statement
    - major gas company credit card billing statement
    - major department store credit card billing statement
    - utility bill (gas, electric, water, sewer, or cable)
    - telephone bill
    - major cell phone service provider
    - active/current insurance declaration page (do not send your insurance card or insurance statement)
    - property tax bill
    - property deed (do not send your property tax receipt)

The second report is the **LexisNexis Full File Disclosure Report.**
- It contains your consumer file and a public records search that includes information available via county, state, and federal public records—real estate transactions and ownership information,

liens, judgments, bankruptcy records, professional licenses, and previous addresses.

- Additional detailed information contained within your full file disclosure report are auto and personal property insurance claims history, current insurance carriers, pre-employment background checks, and criminal records.
- Review <u>frequently asked questions</u> and <u>order your report online</u>.

Check Verification and Checking Account Reports

To review information stored within the checking and deposit account databases, submit requests to the following three companies. Be prepared to provide your name, address, driver's license, and checking account numbers. <u>View a sample checking account history report here.</u> This will allow you to check underwriting history and uncover fraud.

- ➢ <u>Certegy Check Services, Inc.</u> (866-543-6315)
- ➢ <u>Chex Systems, Inc.</u> (800-428-9623)
- ➢ <u>Deposit Payment Protection Services, Inc.</u> (800-262-7771) (uses SCAN—Shared Check Authorization Network)

> You'll notice that the Deposit Payment Protection Services link leads to the Chex Systems Web site. The free annual report request forms and mailing addresses are the same for both companies, but they're ultimately mailed to separate divisions. Simply download the Chex Systems request form <u>here</u> and write the appropriate company name above the address on your mailing label.

Insurance Claims Reports

- These databases contain information on a consumer's five-year claims and payment history for auto, personal property, burglary, credit card theft, worker's compensation, and medical insurance.

- Knowing what's in these reports will help protect you against fraud as well as inaccuracies that could negatively impact your financial reputation.
- ISO is a company that provides insurance claims information to insurance underwriters. Their report is called the Automobile-Property Loss Underwriting Service, or A-PLUS.
- <u>Request a copy of your A-PLUS loss-history report</u> and review its contents. Even if you haven't made any insurance claims in the past five years, a thief may have made claims with your identity. Your report will be mailed within fifteen days. <u>Visit ISO online</u> or call 800-627-3487 to find the office serving you.

Resident History Reports
- Even if you don't rent or haven't rented in years, you should still review your resident history reports.
- Criminals use stolen identities to rent properties, resulting in fraudulent claims of vandalism, eviction, and unpaid rent. It may be some time before it shows up in your credit report or before debt collection agencies show up at your door.
- Your LexisNexis residential history report is included in the full file disclosure report outlined above.
- <u>CoreLogic SafeRent</u> can also supply you with a copy of your tenant and rental history report.

Medical Information Reports
The Medical Information Bureau (MIB) provides information to insurance underwriters about member companies requesting information on consumers, including the specific information requested and a consumer's insurance application history.

- The report discloses usage codes (related to medical conditions or treatments), *not* specific medical details. This information is maintained for seven years.

- Again, even if you haven't applied for insurance underwriting in the past seven years, you should not bypass this review. If you haven't applied and a record exists, it may be an indication of fraud.
- Request your report at the <u>MIB website</u> or by calling 866-692-6901.

Additional Data Brokers

- <u>The Privacy Rights Clearinghouse</u>—a nonprofit consumer information and advocacy corporation—provides valuable information and resources to help you understand your privacy rights and how these data brokers and vendors obtain and provide your information.

Identity Theft Insurance and Credit Monitoring

- Before you choose **credit monitoring** services or **identity theft insurance,** understand that they often have significant limitations and that neither will protect you from becoming a victim.
- Many policies only cover nominal out-of-pocket expenses—photocopying documents, mailing correspondence, and filing fees relative to your case.
- Further limiting coverage are significant deductibles and maximum caps on reimbursements, which may require preapproval by the insurance company.
- Credit monitoring is a limited form of protection that *cannot* protect against criminal, medical, Social Security, tax return, existing account, or synthetic identity fraud.
- Credit monitoring won't alert you if someone obtains employment, a driver's license, a birth certificate, a social security card, or other documents in your name.

Words of Caution

While some identity theft protection and credit monitoring services are legitimate, many are marketing companies skilled at selling fear and a false sense of security. Some businesses claiming to monitor all elements of your identity in "real time" and perform a full recovery if you become a victim have little or no security experience to back it up.

True Story

When Melody Millet contacted a lender to find out why her request for an account to help pay off her auto loan was denied, she was surprised to learn that one already existed under her husband Steve's Social Security number. Mrs. Millet later learned that her husband's Social Security number had been used to apply for twenty-six credit cards, to finance several cars, and to obtain a mortgage. Despite having purchased a credit monitoring service from Equifax, the fraudulent use of Mr. Millet's Social Security number went undetected. The Millets' experience didn't improve even after signing up for credit monitoring with Experian and TransUnion. At least one application for credit using Mrs. Millet's Social Security number was received, yet all of the three credit reporting agencies failed to detect this activity. In fact, the agencies sent the Millets several e-mail messages reassuring them their information was safe. The Millets finally took legal action and sued the credit bureaus.

The Up-sell

Be on the lookout for the "up-sell" scheme. Consumers are initially offered credit monitoring services at low or no base price. The company uses their "proprietary" search tools to watch selected criminal websites. After a short period of time, the client is informed that his or her personal information has been detected on one of those sites, and in order to get complete protection, they must upgrade to a premium package—hence, the up-sell.

Bigger Doesn't Mean Better

One particularly well-known organization has been sued several times for falsely advertising $1 million in identity protection coverage. Customers believing their financial losses would be covered were shocked and disheartened to learn that the $1 million was only applicable to reimburse nominal "out of pocket" expenses like filing, application, copying, and postage fees. Some companies even require victims to prove that the breach was due to a failure in their proprietary search tools before reimbursing funds.

Bottom Line

Service agreements can be complicated and misleading. Get the details in writing, read the fine print, and know what you're paying for.

CHAPTER 6

Recovery

In this chapter, you'll learn what steps to take in the event you suspect fraud or become a victim of identity theft.

Confronting a case of identity theft can be challenging. Successful resolution requires the accurate and timely gathering, organization, tracking, and follow-up of information. Some cases may even require the specialized skills of an attorney or law enforcement professional. In all cases, your liability depends upon how quickly you act. Outlined below are steps you can take in each category if you suspect or discover fraudulent activity.

Taking Action

Take these steps immediately if you suspect fraud.

- Create a case folder containing all correspondence and supporting documentation.
- On the inside cover, attach a data sheet to conveniently and chronologically record all details.
- Include dates, times, types of communication (e.g., notification, follow-up), company representatives with whom you've communicated, and In-depth descriptions of all your discussions.

Disputing ATM, Debit Card, and Credit Card Transactions

- The <u>Electronic Fund Transfer Act (EFTA)</u> highlights your rights and responsibilities regarding ATM and debit card fraud transactions. The <u>Fair Credit Billing Act</u> highlights your rights and responsibilities regarding credit card fraud transactions. The following are examples of billing errors under the FCBA:[2]

> - charges not actually made by the consumer
> - charges in the wrong amount
> - charges for goods or services not received by the consumer
> - charges for goods not delivered as agreed
> - charges for goods that were damaged on delivery
> - failures to properly reflect payments or credits to an account
> - calculation errors
> - charges that the consumer wants clarified or requests proof of
> - statements mailed to the wrong address

- If you detect unauthorized or fraudulent transactions involving your ATM, debit, or credit card, immediately report it to the issuer's fraud department.
- You must follow up your phone notification with a **written letter** detailing the disputed transactions. Keep the originals of all correspondence and send copies to the address provided for billing inquiries, *not* the address for payments. This notice must be mailed within sixty days of the date you received the first statement concerning the fraudulent charge.
- Many major credit card issuers promote "zero liability" for fraudulent transactions involving their ATM or debit cards. There are exceptions, however—most are noted in the fine print of your cardholder agreement. This is why it's imperative to monitor your account regularly and report suspicious activity and lost or stolen cards.
- If lost or stolen cards are reported before any fraudulent transactions take place, you won't be held responsible for those that occur after your notification.

- You may be liable for unauthorized withdrawals with the following liability limits:

  For debit/ATM cards:
  - ➢ Loss is limited to $50 if institution is notified within two business days.
  - ➢ Loss is limited to $500 if institution is notified between three and sixty days.
  - ➢ Loss liability is unlimited if loss is *not r*eported within sixty business days.

  For credit cards:
  - ➢ Loss is limited to $50 if your credit card is used at the point of purchase.
  - ➢ There is no liability if the purchase was made by phone or online.
  - ➢ Loss liability is unlimited if loss is *not r*eported within sixty business days.

- Once the issuing agnecy receives your notification, it has ten days to investigate and must notify you within three days of completing its investigation.
- If the investigation reveals an error or fraud, the issuer must correct the records and replace the funds within one day.
- If the issuer needs additional time to complete its investigation, the EFTA allows another forty-five days—provided the issuer replaces the disputed funds and notifies the consumer that the funds have been credited to his or her account.
- If, at the conclusion of the investigation, the issuer determines that no error or fraud has occurred, the issuer can withdraw the credited funds and notify the consumer with a written explanation of its findings.
- Visit the FTC site for more information on <u>your credit account consumer rights</u>.

Disputing Information on Your Credit Report

Under the <u>Fair Credit Reporting Act (FCRA)</u>, both the credit bureau (e.g., Equifax) and the business that sent the information (e.g., your bank or credit card company) are responsible for correcting fraudulent or inaccurate information in your report. To dispute inaccurate or fraudulent information, notify, **in writing,** all three credit bureaus and any companies or creditors whose information is in question. **Be sure to send all correspondence via certified mail, return receipt requested.** This provides a record that the correspondence was actually delivered. This notification should include the following items:

- a detailed description of the account information and why you believe it to be inaccurate, along with copies of any additional supporting documentation;
- the unique **reference number** appearing on your credit report;
- copies of identification for verification; and
- an identity theft report (if you believe the information disputed is fraudulent).

An **identity theft report** is an extensive police report with enough detail for credit reporting agencies and businesses to verify that you are in fact a victim of identity theft and to determine which inaccurate account information is a result of that theft. It facilitates your rights in the recovery process.

Creating your <u>identity theft report</u>:

1. File a <u>complaint report</u> with the FTC detailing the events of the theft. Once you write and print those details, an **identity theft affidavit** is created. It's a document critical to reporting and resolving fraudulent accounts. The identity theft affidavit includes general information about yourself, the theft, and the account(s) opened or affected in your name.

2. Bring your FTC identity theft affidavit when you file a police report.

3. Together, your FTC identity theft affidavit and your police report make up an **identity theft report**. Be sure to get a copy of the police report or the report number.

*For various reasons, it's not uncommon for victims requesting a police report to get pushback from local law enforcement. Don't get discouraged. Some forget that identity theft is a federal crime that should be treated as such. Be persistent and know that there are additional outlets you can pursue. Any local, state, or federal law enforcement agency is obligated to take your police report. If you still encounter resistance, your state attorney general's office will take it. Print and present <u>this helpful memo to law enforcement</u> (from the FTC) about the importance of creating an identity theft report.

The **information block** process is one way for identity theft victims to manage fraudulent information.

- Upon accepting your identity theft report, the credit bureau has four business days to **block** the fraudulent information in question until it's resolved. Your report is still accessible, just not the information in dispute.
- The credit bureau must notify you and the creditor in writing if it places the block. It must also notify you if it refuses the block.

Reinvestigation is a process designed to help consumers dispute credit report errors or inaccuracies. Contrary to how it sounds, it is actually the initial investigation that follows a dispute.

- Upon accepting a dispute notification from the consumer, the credit bureau is required to investigate. Each has its own procedure.
- The credit bureau must forward your notification, along with all supporting documents and information, to the company reporting the disputed information.
- The creditor must then investigate the matter and report its findings back to the credit bureau. This process usually takes about thirty days.
- If the creditor finds the disputed information to be inaccurate or unverifiable, it must correct or remove that information and notify each of the national credit bureaus.
- The contact information for each agency is listed at the end in the Quick Links Resource Guide. Contact the agency that has reported the inaccurate information to determine its current procedure.

Sample Letters

Access sample letters, forms, and enclosures for victims of identity theft at the FTC Web site, including

- *asking a business to remove fraudulent charges*
- *getting copies of the documents the identity thief used*

Criminal Violations

It's frightening to think someone could commit crimes in your name. Even more disturbing is the fact that you could get arrested for those offenses. Unfortunately, it's a very real threat. In most cases, thieves use fraudulent addresses, and it's only after the victim has a police contact—like a minor traffic infraction—that he or she becomes aware of the impersonation.

- If you become aware of violations falsely committed in your name, contact your state attorney general's office. Procedures for disputing and correcting criminal records vary from state to state.
- Contact the local law enforcement agency that filed the charges on the thief and file a criminal complaint of impersonation.
- Request that the agency take your fingerprints, photograph, and copies of other identifying documents (your driver's license and passport).
- Once your identity has been verified, the law enforcement agency and the local district attorney's office *should* issue some form of a clearance letter or, in the case of an arrest, a certificate of release.
- Monitor the investigation and confirm that any follow-up findings supporting your innocence are filed with the appropriate district attorney's office and court.
- A criminal defense attorney may be required to help fully reconcile your status and correct criminal records filed with prosecutors and law enforcement.

Driver's License ID Theft

- If you suspect that someone has illegally obtained a driver's license in your name, contact your state department or division of motor vehicles (DMV).
- Some states add fraud alerts to your file if you are a victim of identity theft.
- Request your driving record once a year from <u>your state DMV office</u> to proactively detect any fraudulent activity.

Medical Identity Theft

Medical identity theft occurs when someone uses your personal information without your knowledge or consent to obtain, or receive payment for, medical treatment, services, or goods. Victims of medical identity theft may find that their medical records are inaccurate, which can have a serious impact on their ability to obtain proper medical care and insurance benefits.

- If you discover inaccurate information or suspect fraudulent activity in your medical records, request that the health care provider amend the record.
- If the provider created the record in question, it must correct the inaccurate information.
- If the provider disagrees with your claim, submit your statement of disagreement. This statement must be added to your record.
- You can also exercise the following rights under federal law:
  - ➤ the right to request copies of your current medical files from each health care provider;
  - ➤ the right to have your medical records amended to remove inaccurate or incomplete information;
  - ➤ the right to an accounting of disclosures—a record of who has been given access to your medical records—from your health care providers and health insurers, which is very important in tracking down where inaccurate information may have been sent; and
  - ➤ the right to file a complaint with the Office of Civil Rights at the US Department of Health and Human Services, if a health care provider does not comply with these rights.

In addition, many hospitals have patient advocates who may be able to help you obtain medical records and access information. Review your rights in greater detail at the Department of Health & Human Services site.

Phone Fraud

- If you suspect that an account for phone service has been fraudulently opened in your name, contact the service provider immediately and cancel the account.
- Open a new account using a different PIN for access.
- If you experience any difficulty having the fraudulent charges removed by your service provider, the following agencies can assist you:
  - For local service, contact your state's Public Utility Commission.
  - For cellular phones and long distance, contact the Federal Communications Commission (FCC), 1-888-CALL-FCC.

Mail Fraud

- If you suspect mail theft or tampering, notify the US Postal Inspection Service (USPIS) immediately and file a complaint.
- Locate your USPIS district office online or by calling your local post office.

Passport Fraud

 A US passport is very valuable to a thief, or worse—a terrorist. Take extra precautions to secure your passport abroad and at home.

- If you believe your passport is lost, stolen, or used fraudulently, contact the US Department of State (USDS).

- When not traveling, secure your passport in a safe or secure file cabinet.
- When traveling, make a color copy of your passport's first page and store it away from the original in case it's ever lost or stolen.
- You can also scan and save a copy in an e-mail or a cloud computing folder like <u>Dropbox</u>, which allows you to store virtual files online and access them from virtually anywhere by connecting to the online service if the original is lost or stolen.
- Thefts of American tourist passports are on the rise. Take the necessary precautions to protect yours.

— CHAPTER 7 —
Know Your Rights

This chapter highlights important federal laws and regulations enacted to protect you against and guide you through the repercussions of identity fraud. We'll outline your key rights and provide links to further resources.

The following laws will help you in these areas:

- empower you to advocate on your own behalf
- relate to the storing, sharing, and reporting of your credit and personal information
- provide free access to the reports that credit bureaus and data aggregating companies use when providing your personal information
- place certain responsibilities on these providers and creditors to correct or remove inaccurate and/or fraudulent information from your credit report
- require businesses to be more transparent in their advertising

The Fair Credit Reporting Act (FCRA) regulates the collection, dissemination, and use of consumer information. Enforced by the US Federal Trade Commission (FTC), it promotes the accuracy, fairness, and privacy of information maintained in credit bureau files and lays the foundation for consumer credit rights in the US.

- You must be told if information in your file has been used against you (e.g., to deny you a loan).
- Access to your file is generally very limited.
- Your consent is required for reports provided to employers.

- You have a right to know what's in your credit file.
- You can request your credit files at any time upon providing proper identification. This is known as your **file disclosure.**
- You have a right to know your credit score.
- You can dispute inaccurate information contained in your credit report.
- You can delete outdated information.
- You can remove your name from marketing lists for unsolicited credit and insurance offers.
- You're entitled to free reports if any of these terms are met:
  - ➤ if incorrect information in the report has caused adverse consequences because you are a victim of identity theft or fraud;
  - ➤ if you're receiving public assistance; or
  - ➤ if you are unemployed and plan on seeking employment within sixty days.

The **Fair and Accurate Credit Transaction Act (FACTA) of 2003** was passed as an amendment to the Fair Credit Reporting Act (FCRA) to further reduce identity theft and provide additional rights for consumers. Key provisions are noted below.

- You're entitled to one free credit report every twelve months from each credit bureau.
- Additional free copies are available to those who suspect fraud.
- Victims of identity theft can place fraud alerts in their credit files, while active duty military personnel can place active duty alerts in theirs. These alerts require creditors to take additional steps in verifying the identity of applicants before issuing credit.
- You're entitled to add a credit freeze. (If you're a victim, it's free. If not, states may charge a small fee.)
- A credit bureau requested to place a fraud alert on a consumer's account must notify the other two credit agencies.

- Once a fraud alert is placed, the file is removed from pre-screened lists for two years.
- Businesses must shorten—or truncate—your account information on electronically printed receipts. Showing more than five digits of the card number or the expiration date of the card on the consumer's copy is strictly prohibited.
- When requested by the consumer, credit bureaus must not print more than the last four digits of a consumer's social security number in a requested credit report.
- Credit bureaus must notify identity theft victims of their rights.
- Credit bureaus must notify identity theft victims of fraud alerts placed on their files.
- Victims have the right to block information in their reports resulting from fraud.
- Victims have the right to obtain copies of documents used to commit fraud.
- You have the right to dispute inaccuracies with creditors directly, rather than initiating a dispute with the credit bureaus in question. (Creditors are not required to check with credit agencies before issuing credit, and not all creditors report the extension of credit to the agencies.)

The Fair Debt Collection Practices Act (FDCPA) establishes guidelines for collection agencies seeking legitimate debts from non-victims and provides protection for consumers against unfair, deceptive, or abusive practices.

- The following debt collection practices are **prohibited:**
  - ➤ calling before 8:00 a.m. or after 9:00 p.m.
  - ➤ calling repeatedly with the intent to annoy or harass

> ➤ calling you at your place of employment after being notified not to, or being made aware that this type of contact violates your employer's policy
> ➤ using obscenities, racial slurs, or insults
> ➤ contacting you knowing that you have legal representation
> ➤ contacting you after a written request to cease contact has been sent

Communication is allowed to advise the consumer that collection efforts are being terminated or that legal action is being pursued.

> ➤ using deceit or misrepresentation to collect a debt (e.g., a collector using phony stationary to impersonate an official court or government notice)
> ➤ accept a post-dated check and deposit it prematurely
> ➤ falsifying or misrepresenting your debt in any way
> ➤ publishing your name or address on a "bad debt list" or otherwise notifying others (e.g., friends, family, and neighbors) that you owe a debt

Debt collectors *can* attempt to contact neighbors and co-workers, but only to obtain information about your location.

> ➤ threatening arrest or legal action that is not permitted or not legitimately being considered
> ➤ threatening to report false information to a credit reporting agency

- It is a **mandatory requirement** for a debt collector to do the following things:
  > ➤ identify him/herself as a debt collector in every communication

➢ state that any information obtained will be used for the purpose of collecting a debt

➢ send a written notification to the consumer within five days of the first communication stating who the collector is, for whom he or she is collecting, and the amount owed

➢ inform you of your right to dispute the debt, in part or in full, and of your right to request that the collector validate the debt within thirty days of receiving notice

➢ provide verification of the debt once a consumer requests validation

➢ notify the relative credit bureaus if you choose to dispute the debt

➢ refrain from intentionally pressuring you to respond to any lawsuit

The collector is only allowed to file a lawsuit where the consumer lives or where the contract was signed.

• Report the conduct of debt collectors to the <u>Federal Trade Commission</u> or your <u>state attorney general's office.</u>
• View the full version of the <u>Fair Debt Collectors Practices Act</u> for more information.

The Identity Theft and Assumption Deterrence Act of 1998 officially designated identity theft as a federal crime, assigning resources of federal law enforcement agencies like the Secret Service, FBI, US Postal Inspection Service, and Social Security Administration's Office of the Inspector General to investigate and prosecute identity theft complaints.

• It is the law that made identity theft a federal crime, which allows the resources of federal law enforcement agencies to investigate and prosecute.

- It also established the Federal Trade Commission as a central agency responsible for mitigating complaints and referrals and for providing resources to identity theft victims.
- As mandated by the act, the FTC established a central repository known as the Consumer Sentinel Database, which accepts and tracks reported incidents of identity theft. This database also maintains the US national repository of identity theft complaints, known as the Identity Theft Data Clearinghouse.
- View the full version of the Identity Theft Assumption and Deterrence Act for more information.

The rights provided to consumers under these laws do not cover your medical records or information contained in them. HIPAA provides some privacy protections, but weaknesses—like the lack of a central repository for medical information—make it difficult to correct inaccurate or fraudulent information.

Additional Federal Rights

On October 30, 2004, President George W. Bush signed into law the Justice For All Act, establishing additional rights for victims of crime whose cases are prosecuted in federal court. For identity theft victims, the act grants the following rights:

- to be reasonably protected from the accused;
- to reasonable, accurate, and timely notice of any public court proceeding, any parole proceeding involving the crime, or any release or escape of the accused;
- not to be excluded from any such public court proceeding unless the court determines that the identity theft victim's testimony would be materially altered if he or she heard other testimony at that proceeding;

- to be reasonably heard at any public proceeding within the district court involving release, plea, sentencing, or parole;
- to confer with the government attorney for the case;
- to full and timely restitution, as provided by law;
- to proceedings free from unreasonable delay; and
- to be treated with fairness and respect for his or her dignity and privacy.

Additional State Rights

Many states have taken proactive measures, passing specific laws to enforce even greater protections for consumers. You may have additional rights under these laws. Contact your state attorney general's office to learn more.

Your Call to Action

Action is a great restorer and builder of confidence.
Inaction is not only the result, but the cause of fear.
— *Norman Vincent Peale*

You are now well aware of the serious consequences of identity theft. You are aware that it is a global problem, with criminals, both domestic and foreign, actively engaged in using personal information to commit fraud.

The ultimate guardian of your identity is *you*. This guide offers techniques for reducing your risk of becoming an identity theft victim, but those techniques only work when applied. Don't rely on anyone or anything outside yourself to keep you safe. Your security is determined not only by what you do, but also by what you *don't* do. Take the simple measures I've outlined to implement good security habits in your daily life and develop a solid security plan based not on hope, but on proven methods.

Taking an active role in protecting your identity is not only prudent—it's patriotic. Each American who secures his or her identity raises the bar for criminals and terrorists. By not protecting yourself, you're essentially leaving the window open and encouraging the cycle. You can make a difference. Seize the opportunity to protect yourself, your family, and our great country by starting your identity lockdown now!

Aside from being morally reprehensible, identity theft is a federal crime that carries penalties of up to fifteen years' imprisonment and a maximum fine of $250,000. If you have any information relating to fraudulent behavior, report it anonymously to the Federal Trade Commission (FTC), the FBI, or your state's attorney general.

Quick Links Resource Guide

Below is a list of clickable online resources, many of which I called upon to complete this guide. Each resource is hyperlinked to its corresponding website. With a working Internet connection, simply click to visit the resource online or hover to view its web address.

CREDIT REPORTS - Orders
- **Equifax, TransUnion, Experian**
- **Innovis:** Download the credit report request form and mail to this address:

    Innovis
    Attention: Consumer Assistance
    PO Box 1358
    Columbus, OH 43216-1358

Credit Reports: Disputes
- **Experian**
- **Equifax**
- **Transunion**
- **Innovis**

Government Resources
- **Fair Credit Reporting Act and Fair and Accurate Credit Transaction Act (FCRA, FACTA)**
    - **FBI: A Parent's Guide to Internet Safety**
    - **FBI: Field Office Locator**
- **Federal Bureau of Investigations (FBI)**
- **Federal Communications Commission (FCC): Online Complaints**
- **Federal Trade Commission (FTC)**

- o FTC Affidavit Form
- o FTC Course of Action Chart
- o FTC Identity Theft Resource Center
- o FTC Memo to Law Enforcement
- o FTC Safeguarding Your Child's Future
- Identity Theft Assumption and Deterrence Act (ITADA)
- Internal Revenue Service (IRS)
- Social Security Administration (SSA): Complaints
- State Attorney General Offices (National Association of Attorneys General)
- The Fair Debt Collection Practices Act (FDCPA)
- US Department of State: Passport Information
- US Postal Inspection Service
- US Secret Service: Take Charge Fact Sheet
- US Securities and Exchange Commission (SEC)
- US Securities and Exchange Commission: Complaints

General
- Privacy Rights Clearinghouse
- Identity Theft Resource Center
- Javelin Strategy and Research

Medical Resources
- Health Information Privacy
- How to File a Patient Safety Confidentiality Complaint
- Medical Information Bureau (MIB): Medical Underwriting History
- World Privacy Forum
- Center on Medical Record Rights And Privacy
- US Department of Health and Human Services Office for Civil Rights

Marketing Resources
- **Direct Marketing Association**
- **Do Not Call Registry**
- **Opt-Out Preapproved Credit Offers**
- **Register a Complaint with the FTC Regarding Telemarketers**

Protection Resources
- **Home PC Firewall Guide: PC Security Links**
- Safe Password Assistance
  - http://www.safepasswd.com
  - www.howsecureismypassword.net

Personal Information and History
- **Certegy: Checking History**
- **CoreLogic SafeRent: Rental History**
- **Full File Disclosure**
- **ISO: Insurance Claims History**
- **LexisNexis: Accurint Person Report**
- **State Listing of Department of Motor Vehicles**

Bibliography

Alvarez, Lizette, "ID Thieves Loot Tax Checks, Filing Early and Often," *New York Times,* May 26, 2012, accessed May 27, 2012.

Baker, Marie; Frederick, Jonathan; CERT. "Keeping Your Family Safe in a Highly Connected World." *Cert.org.* Software Engineering Institute, Carnegie Mellon University, Aug. 2011. Web. Jan. 2013.

Bureau of Consumer Protection Business Center. "Medical Identity Theft: FAQs for Health Care Providers and Health Plans." *Business.ftc. gov.* Federal Trade Commission, Jan. 2011. Web. Jan. 2013.

Dixon, Pam, World Privacy Forum. "Medical Identity Theft: The Information Crime That Can Kill You." *Worldprivacyforum.org.* World Privacy Forum, 3 May 2006. Web. 28 May 2012.

"Fair and Accurate Credit Transactions Act of 2003 (FACTA)." *FTC*.gov. Federal Trade Commission, n.d. Web. Jan. 2013.

"Fair Credit Reporting Act (FCRA)." *FTC.gov.* Federal Trade Commission, n.d. Web. Jan, 2013.

"Fair Debt Collection Practices Act (FDCPA)." *FTC*.gov. Federal Trade Commission, n.d. Web. Jan, 2013.

Federal Bureau of Investigation. "Safety and Security for US Students Traveling Abroad." *Fbi.gov.* FBI, US Department of Justice, n.d. Web. Dec. 2012.

Federal Trade Commission. "Identity Theft and Assumption Deterrence Act of 1998." *Ftc*.gov. FTC, n.d. Web. Jan. 2013.

Federal Trade Commission. "Safeguarding Your Child's Future." *Ftc.gov.* FTC, Aug. 2012. Web. Dec. 2012.

Federal Trade Commission. "Taking Charge: What To Do If Your Identity Is Stolen." *Ftc.gov.* FTC, April 2013. Web. Nov. 2012.

Javers, Eamon. CNBC. Tax Scam: IRS Pays Out Billions in Fraudulent Refunds." *CNBC.com.* CNBC, 2 Aug. 2012. Web. Jan. 2013.

Jayaraman, Kavita; Blank, Phil. Javelin Strategy & Research. "2012 Identity Fraud Report: Consumers Taking Control to Reduce Their Risk of Fraud." *Idmax.com.* Javelin Strategy & Research, Feb. 2012. Web. Dec. 2012.

Miceli, Danielle; Kim, Rachel. Javelin Strategy & Research. "2010 Identify Fraud Survey Report: Consumer Version." *Javelinstrategy.com.* Javelin Strategy & Research, Feb. 2010. Web. Dec. 2012.

Ponemon Institute. "Third Annual Survey on Medical Identity Theft." *Ponemon.org.* Ponemon Institute, June 2012. Web. Jan. 2013.

Power, Richard. Carnegie Mellon CyLab. "Child Identity Theft." *Cylab. cmu.edu.* Carnegie Mellon CyLab, n.d. Web. Dec. 2012.

Sileo, John D. *Privacy Means Profit, Prevent Identity Theft and Secure You and Your Bottom Line.* New Jersey: John Wiley & Sons, Inc., 2010.

Social Security Administration. "Identity Theft and Your Social Security Number." *Socialsecurity.gov.* SSA, Oct 2012. Web. Jan. 2013.

Social Security Administration. "Your Social Security Number and Card." *Socialsecurity.gov.* SSA, Aug 2012. Web. Jan. 2013.

Vander Nat, Peter; Rothstein, Paul. Federal Trade Commission. "Report to Congress under Section 319 of the Fair and Accurate Credit Transaction Act of 2003." *Ftc.gov*. Federal Trade Commission, Dec. 2010. Web. Dec. 2012.

About the Author

James R. LaPiedra, CFP®, CITRMS®, has twenty-eight years of management experience in both the public and private sectors. With over twenty years as a highly decorated veteran of the New York City Police Department, Jim served as the commander of several investigative and patrol units before retiring in 2000 as a deputy inspector.

Beyond his tenure with the NYPD, Jim served as network security manager for the former online brokerage firm DLJDirect, as well as senior security manager for Lehman Brothers, where as senior vice president, he directed security operations for North and South America.

Jim is the president and CEO of ID360°, an identity theft risk management and recovery provider. He holds the Certified Identity Theft Risk Management Specialist (CITRMS®) designation and is a frequent presenter at identity theft seminars and workshops. He's developed an identity lockdown program for clients that minimizes risk and provides a recovery process in the event that their identities become compromised.

Jim is also a CERTIFIED FINANCIAL PLANNER™ professional who specializes in retirement planning and distribution strategies. He has a BBA in accounting from St. John's University and holds general securities and investment adviser representative licenses, as well as life, accident, and health insurance licenses.

Jim LaPiedra is available for corporate and group speaking engagements, consulting, and identity theft education services. For more information visit info@yourid360.com.

Jim LaPiedra, ID360°, and the information contained in this manual, does not officially endorse any product, service, or entity.